Real World
Colouring Book
For Advanced Users & Adults

50 Images

Created From Real Life Photos
For You To Colour As You Please.

ISBN 978-0-359-83294-1
90000
9 780359 832941

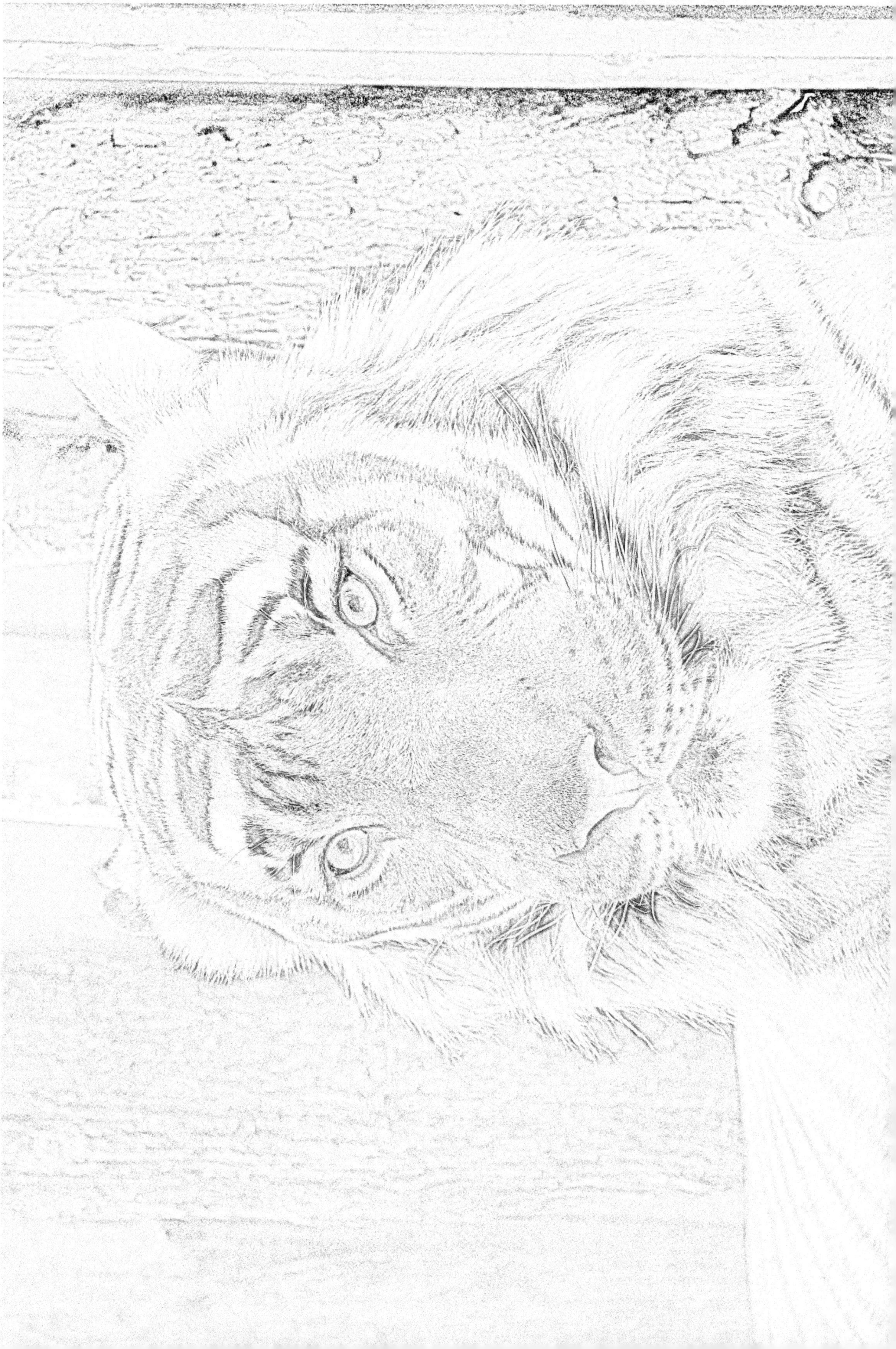

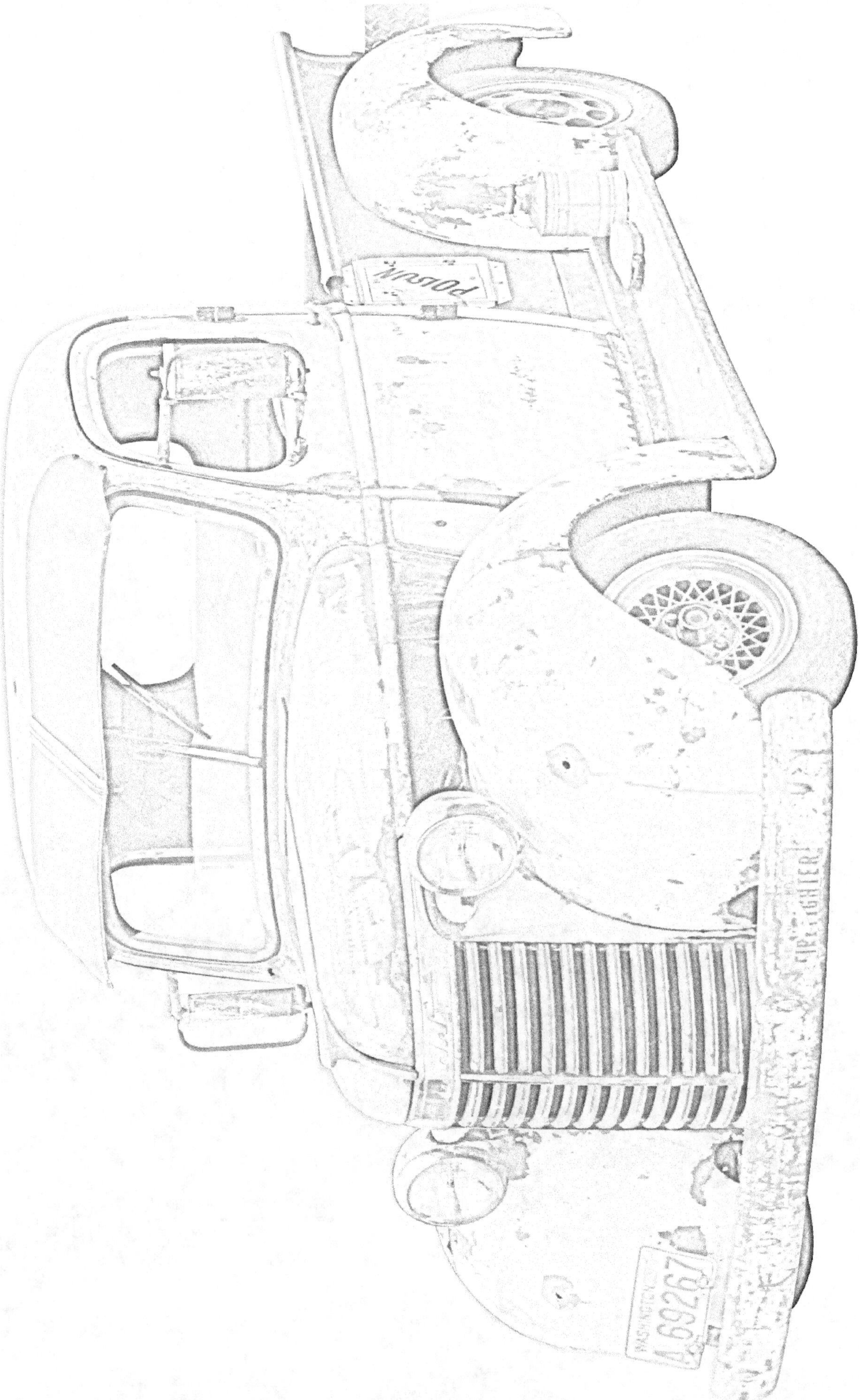

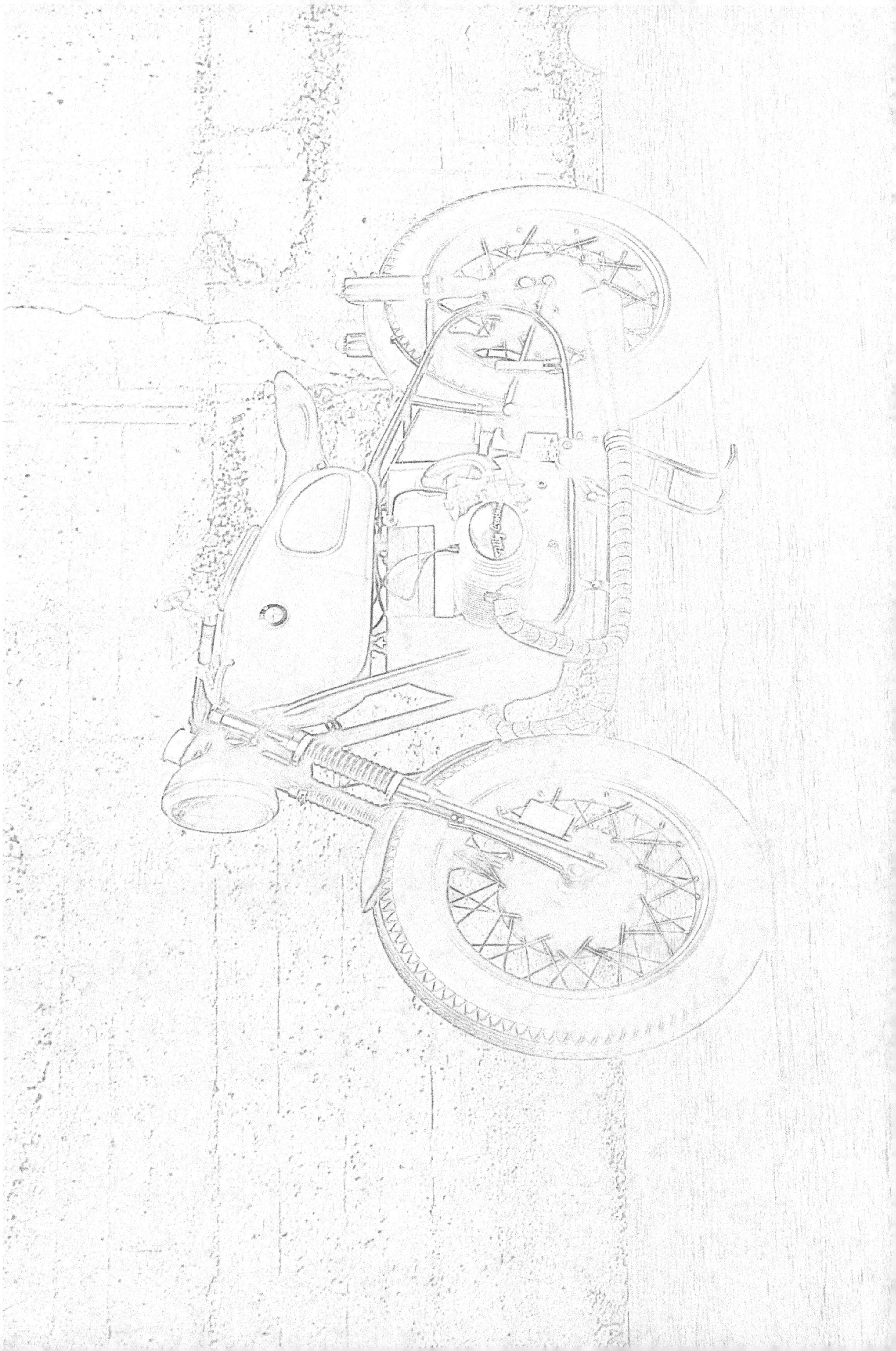

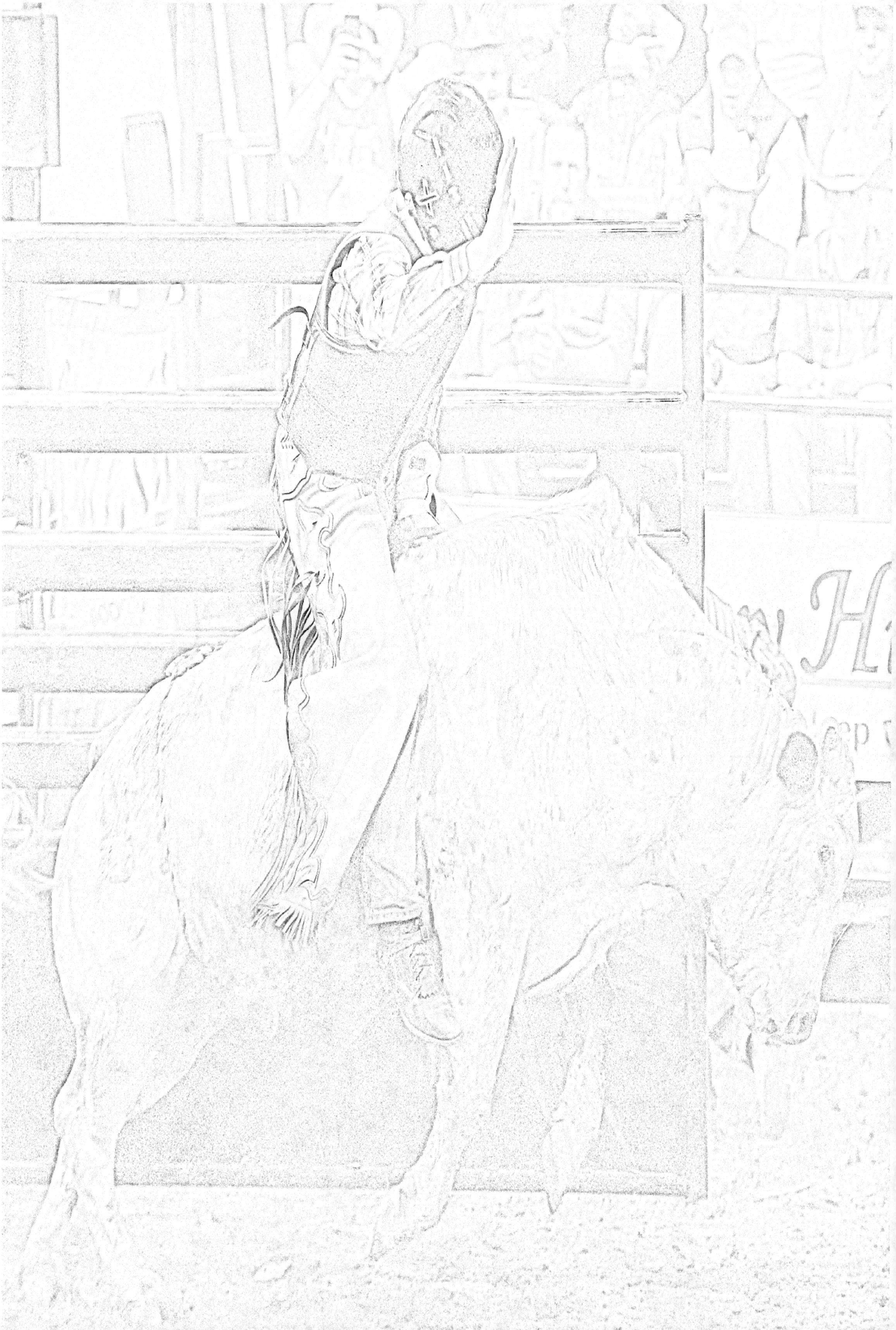

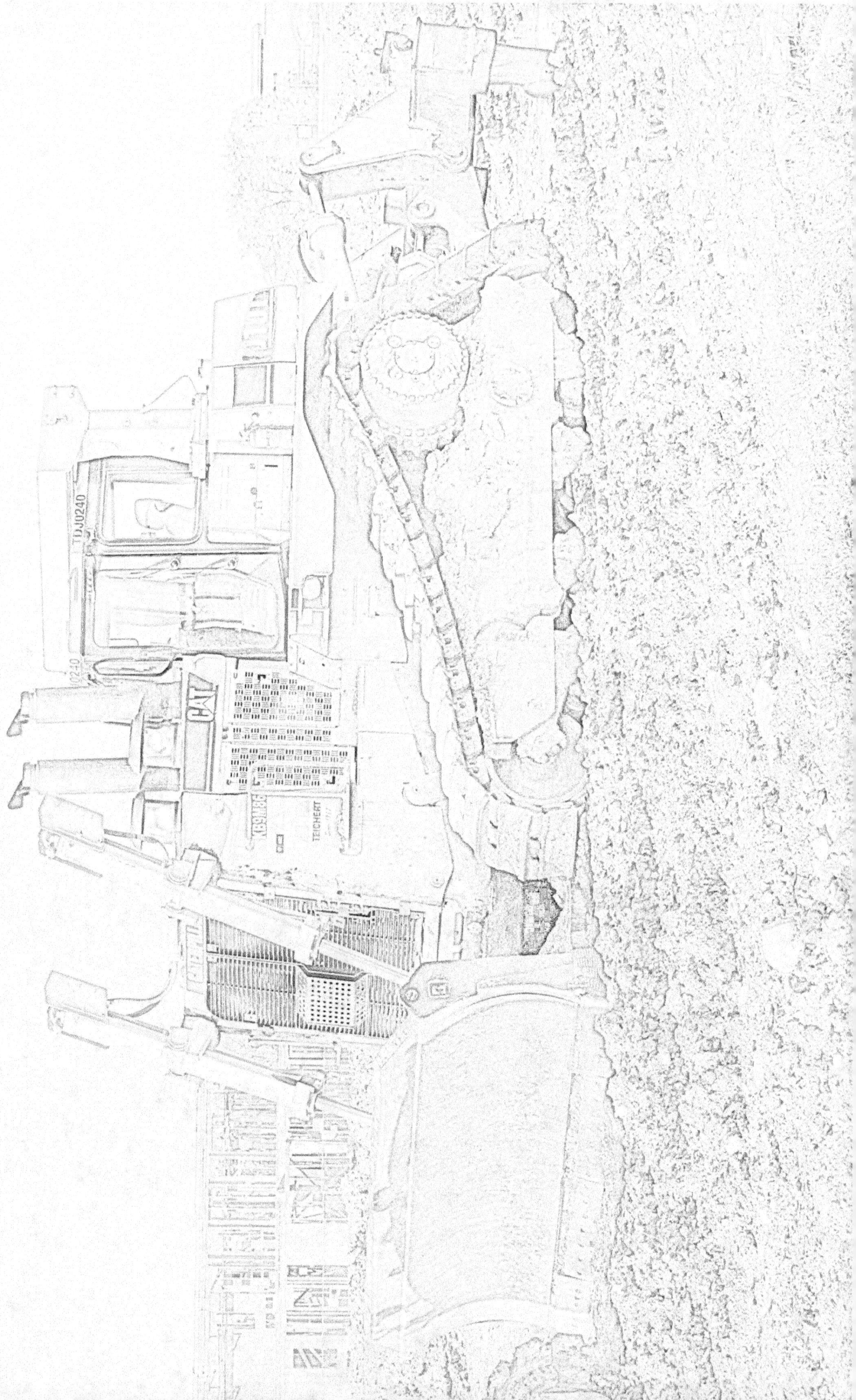
TDJ0240
CAT
TEICHERT

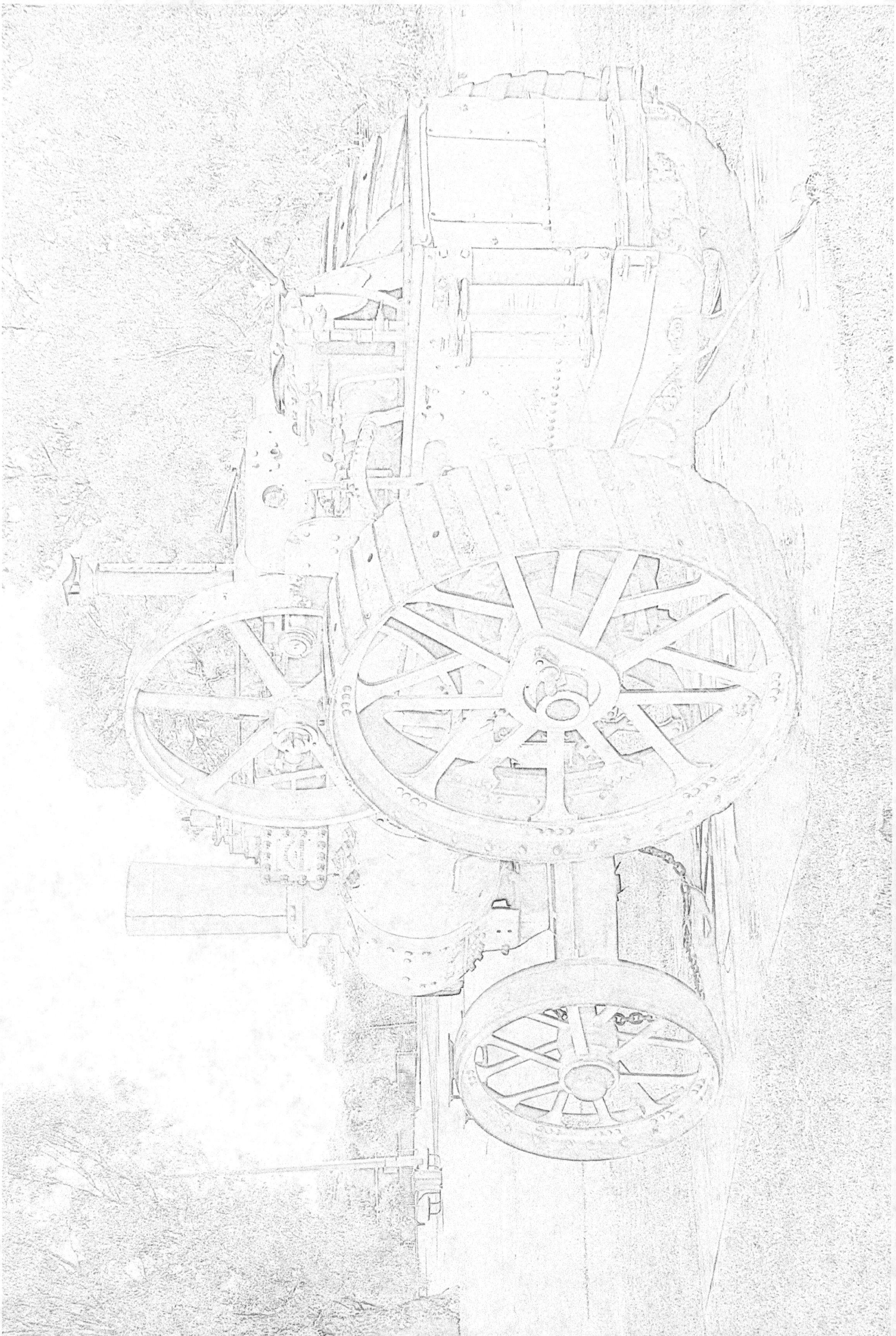

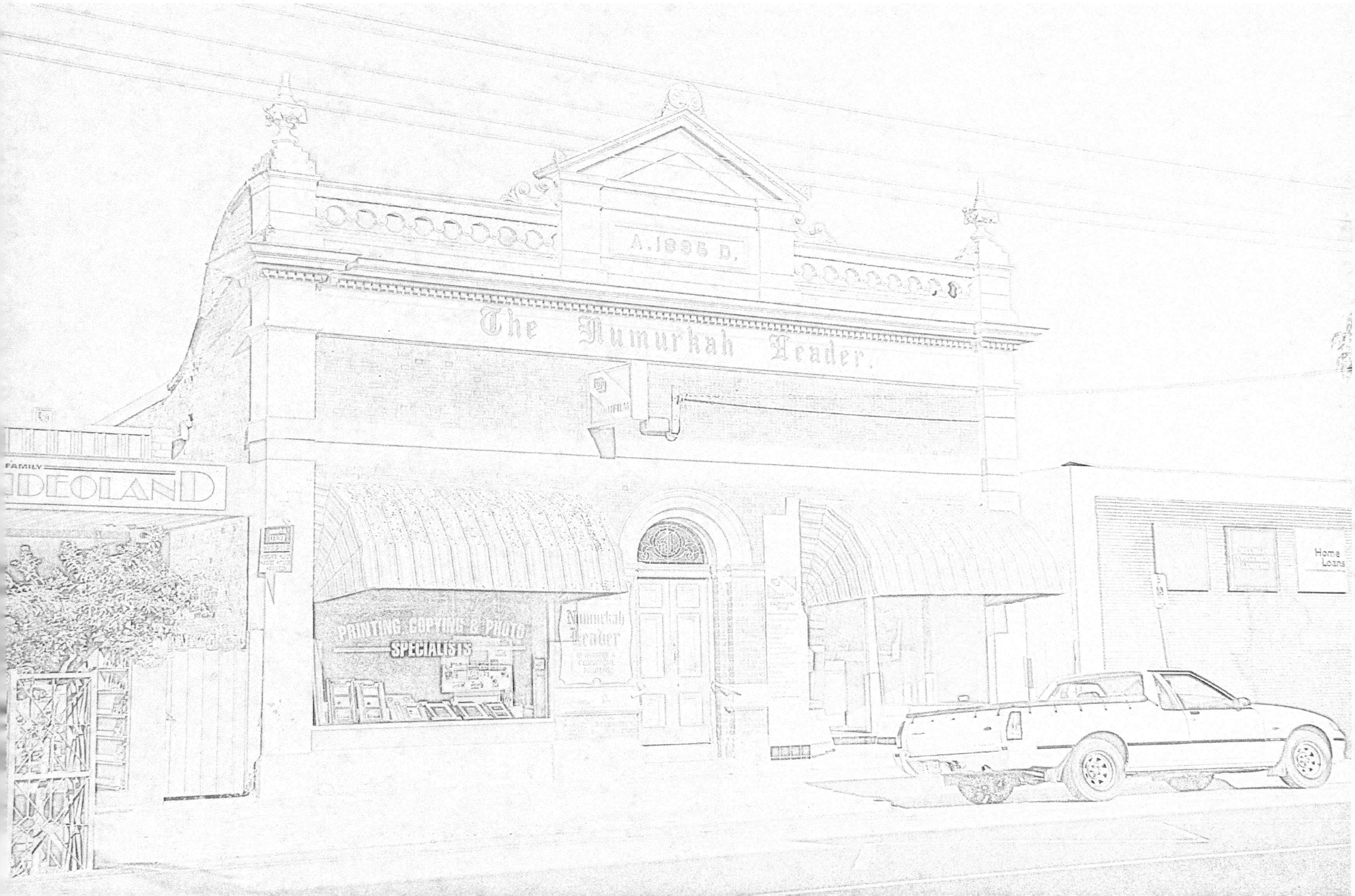
The Numurkah Leader
FAMILY
PRINTING COPYING & PHOTO
SPECIALISTS
Numurkah Leader
Home Loans

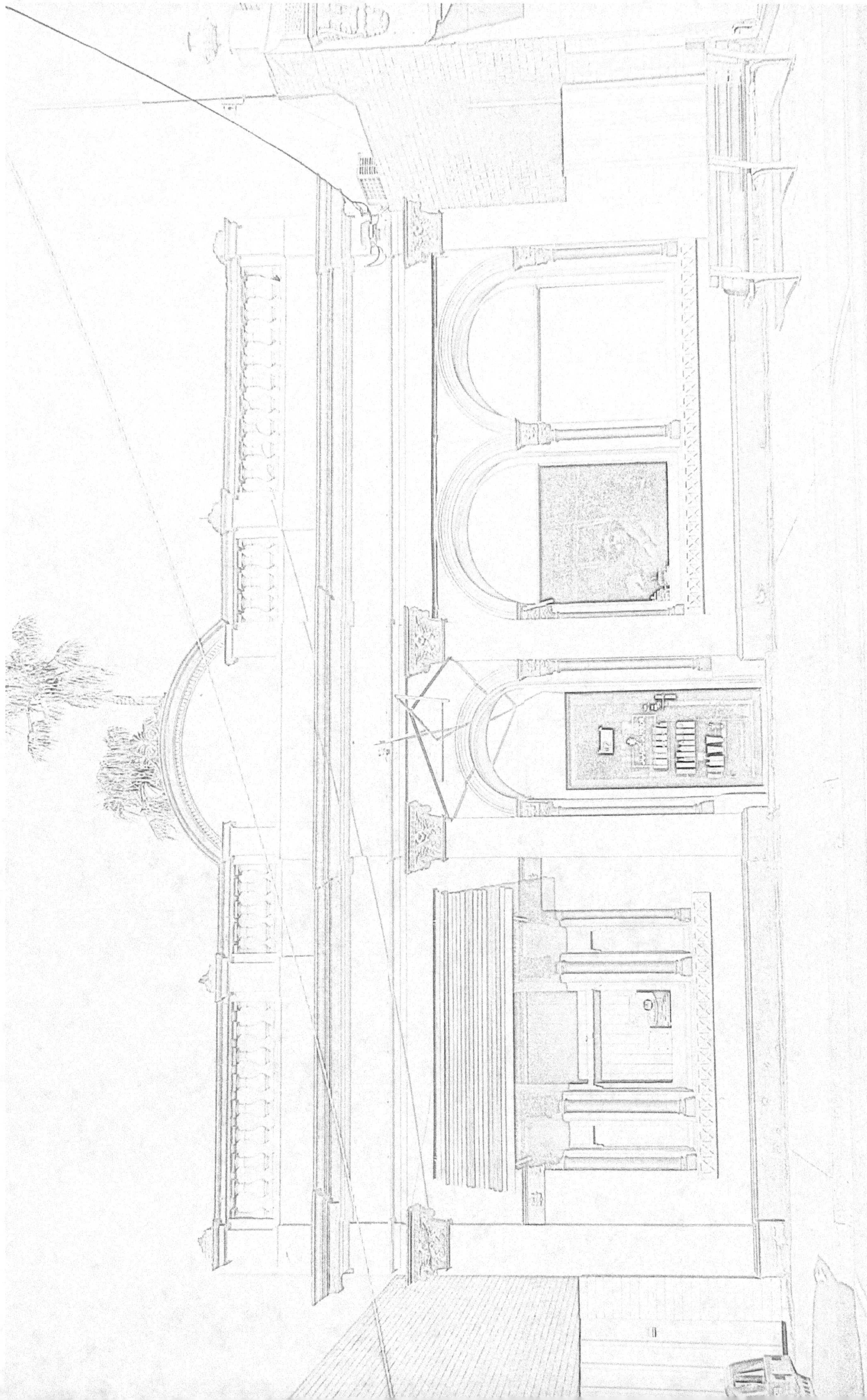

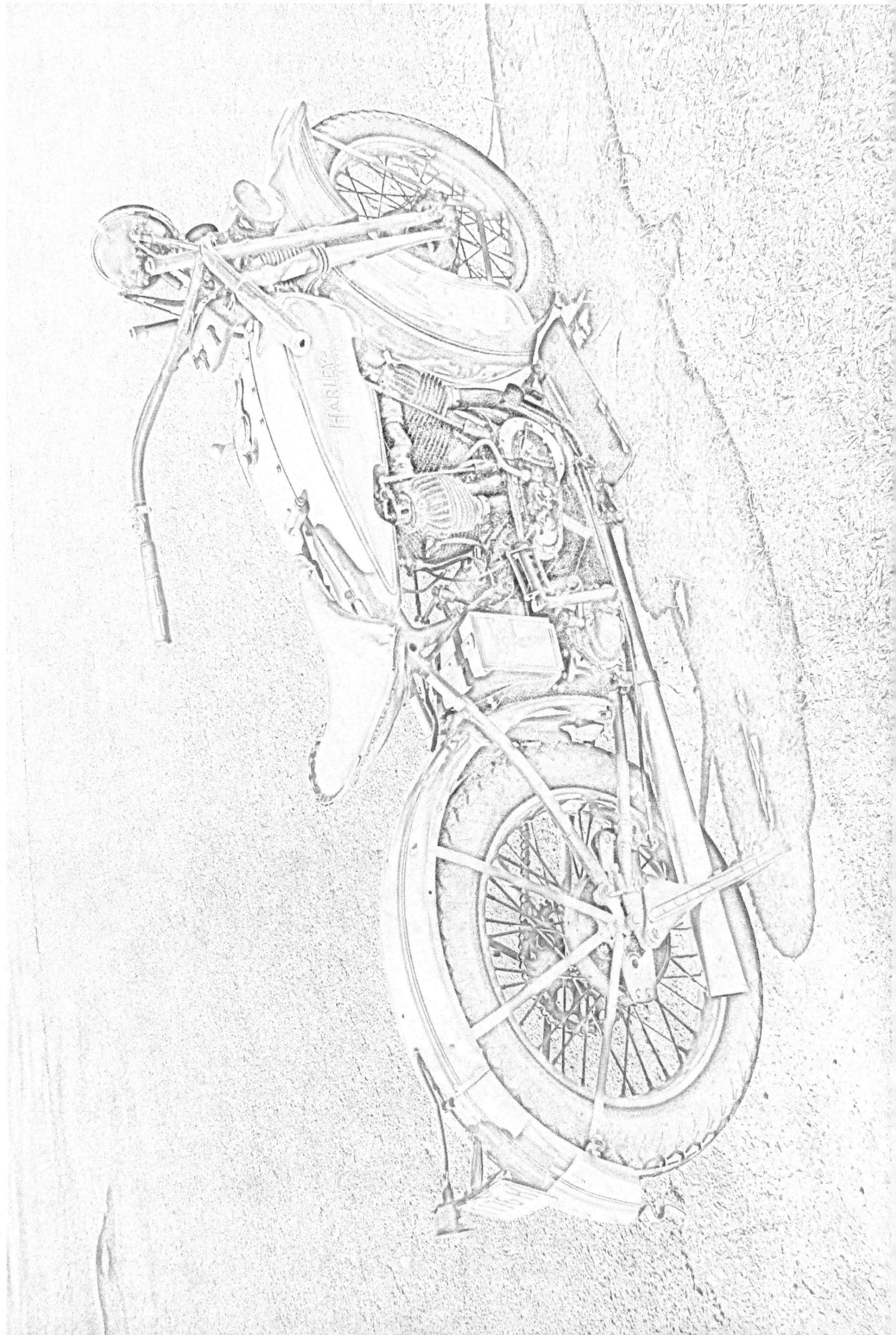
HARLEY-

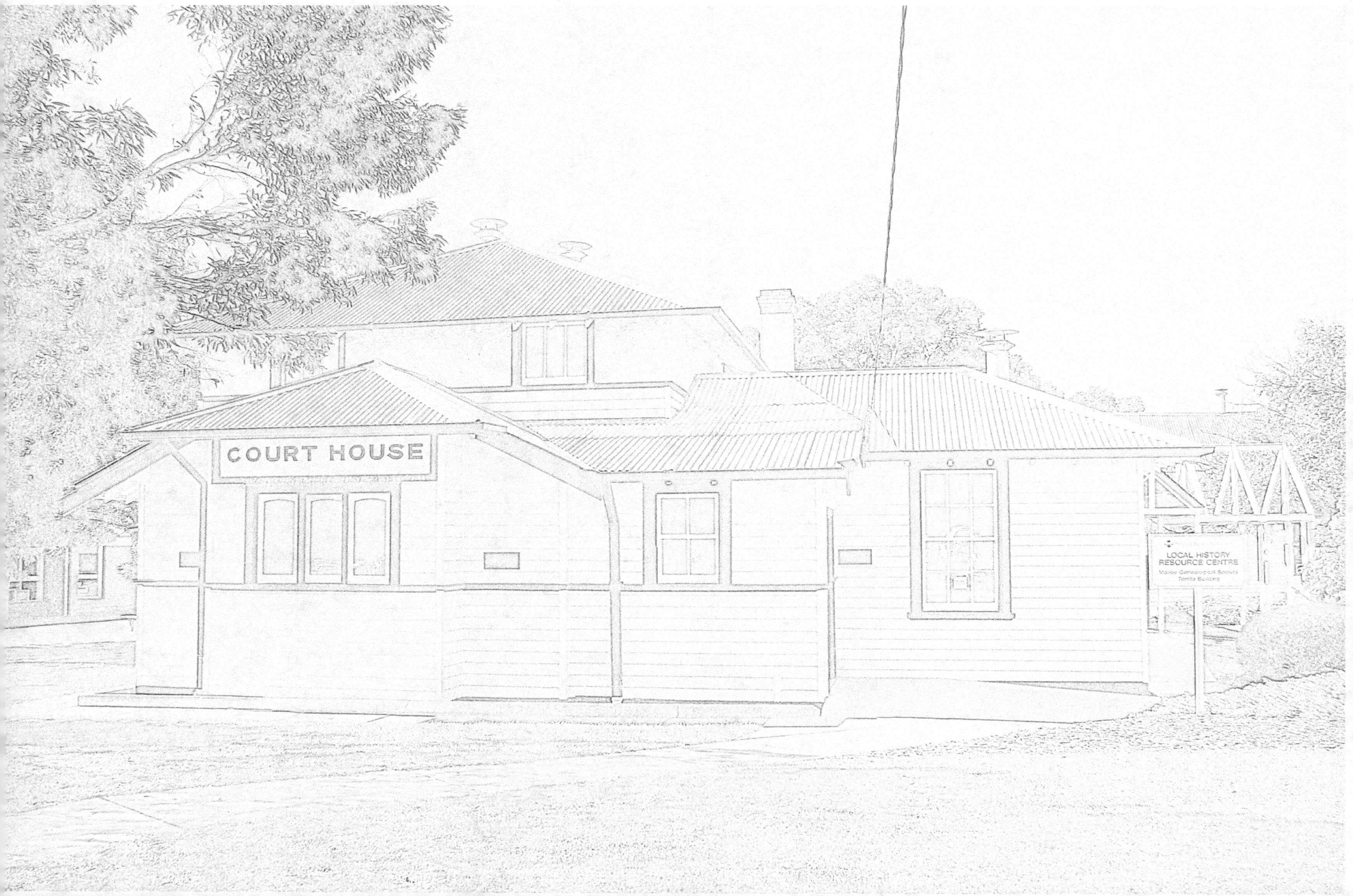
COURT HOUSE
LOCAL HISTORY
RESOURCE CENTRE

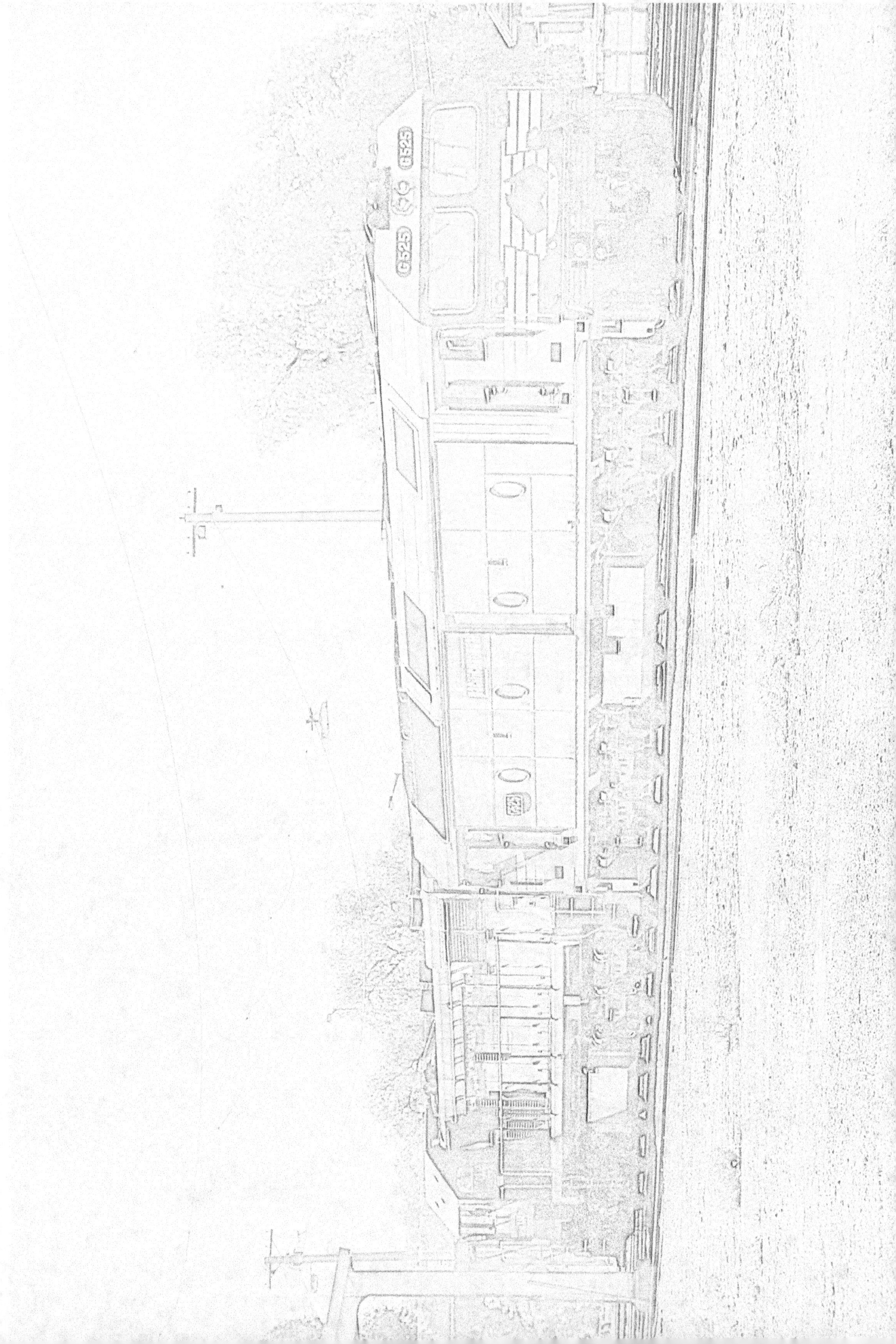
G525

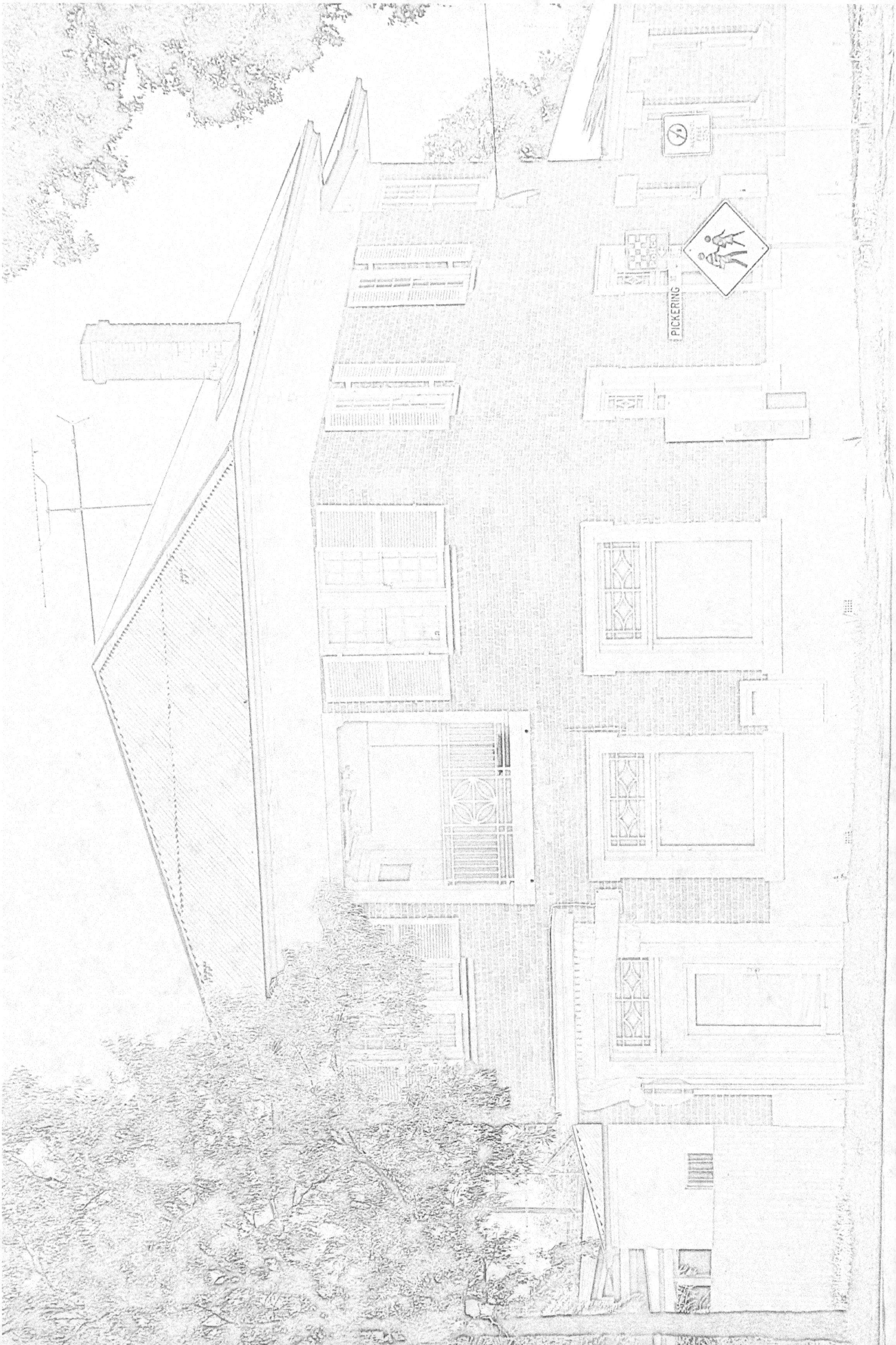
PICKERING

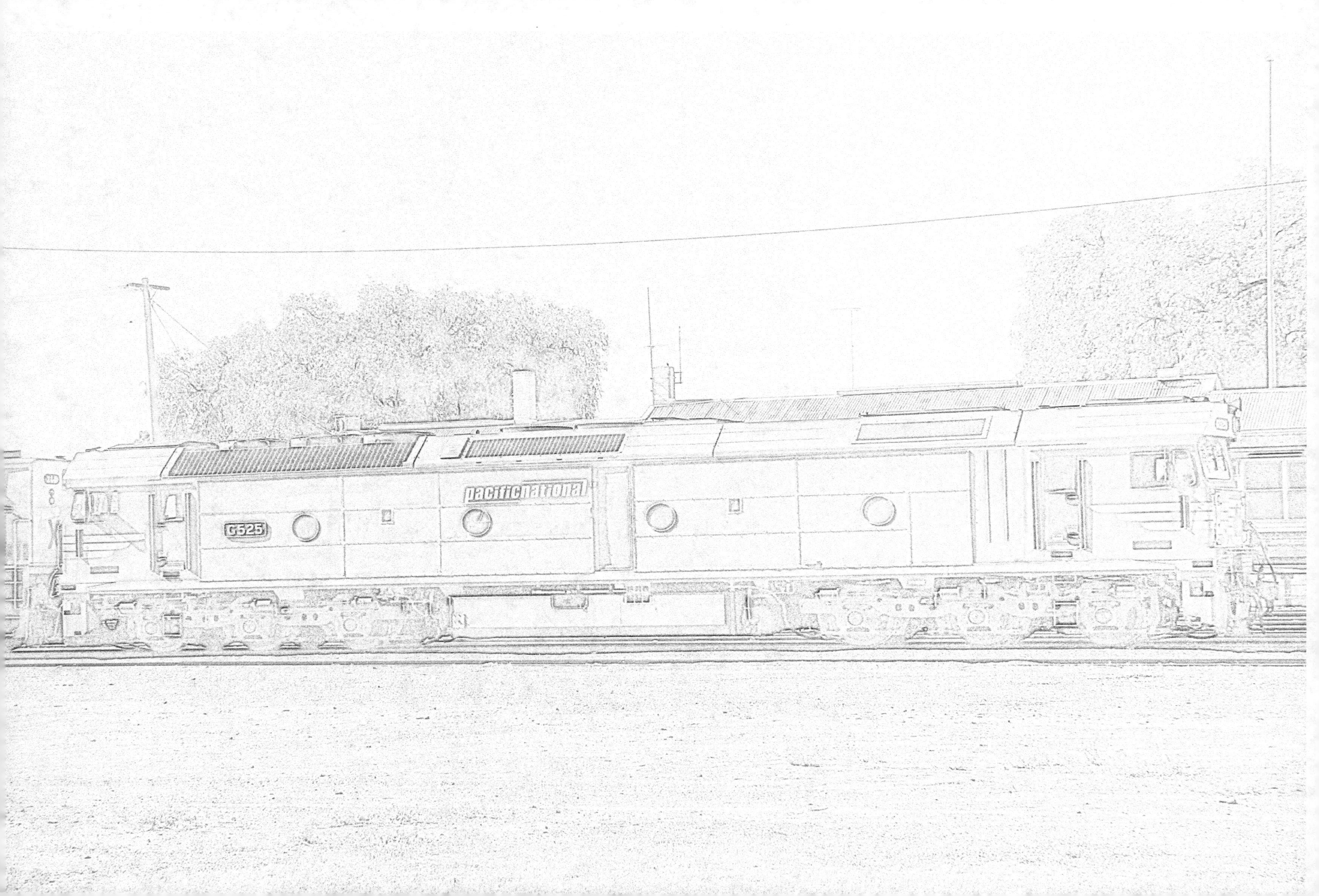
G525
pacificnational

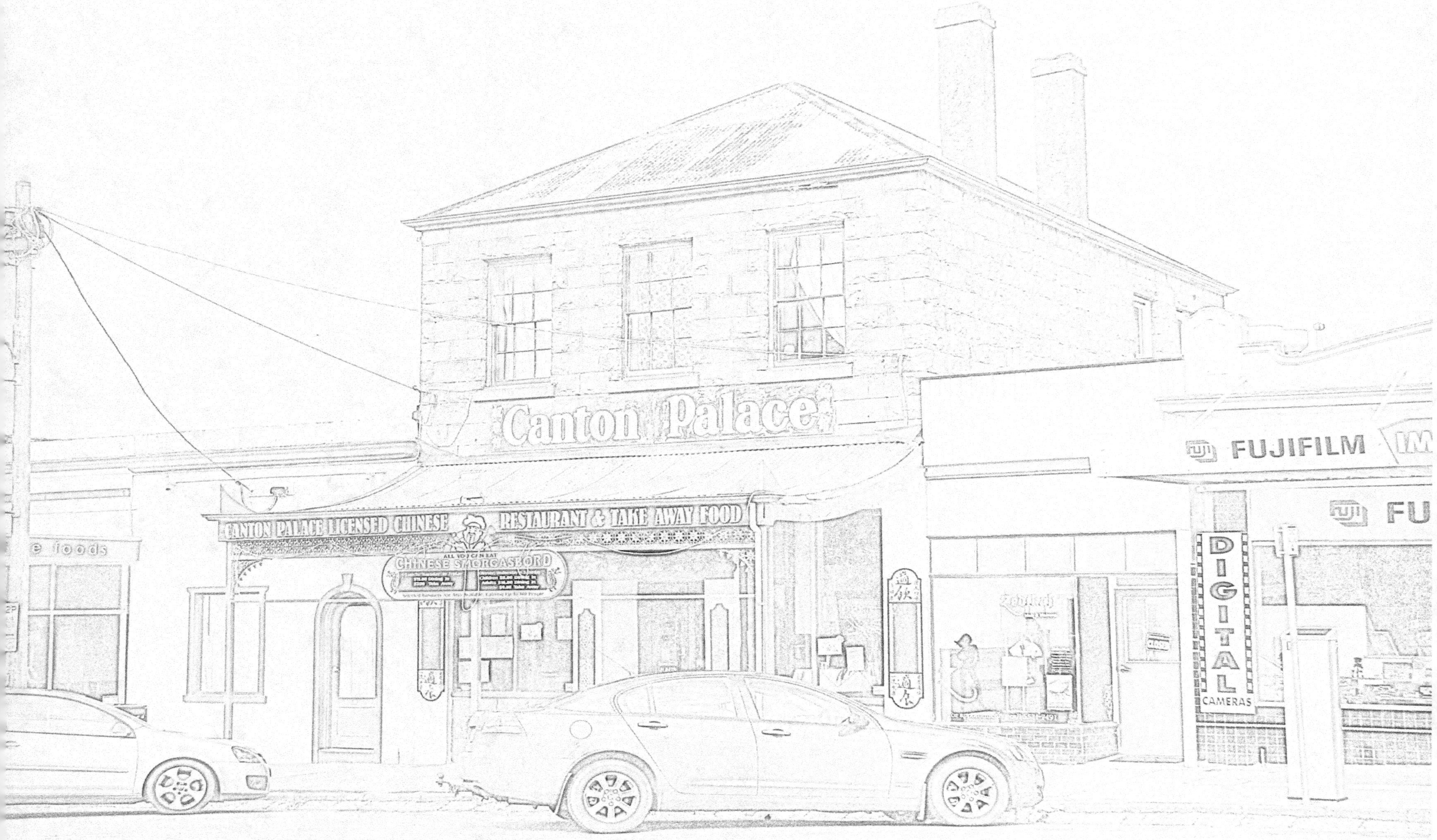
Canton Palace
CANTON PALACE LICENSED CHINESE
RESTAURANT & TAKE AWAY FOOD
ALL YOU CAN EAT
CHINESE SMORGASBORD
FUJIFILM
DIGITAL
CAMERAS
foods

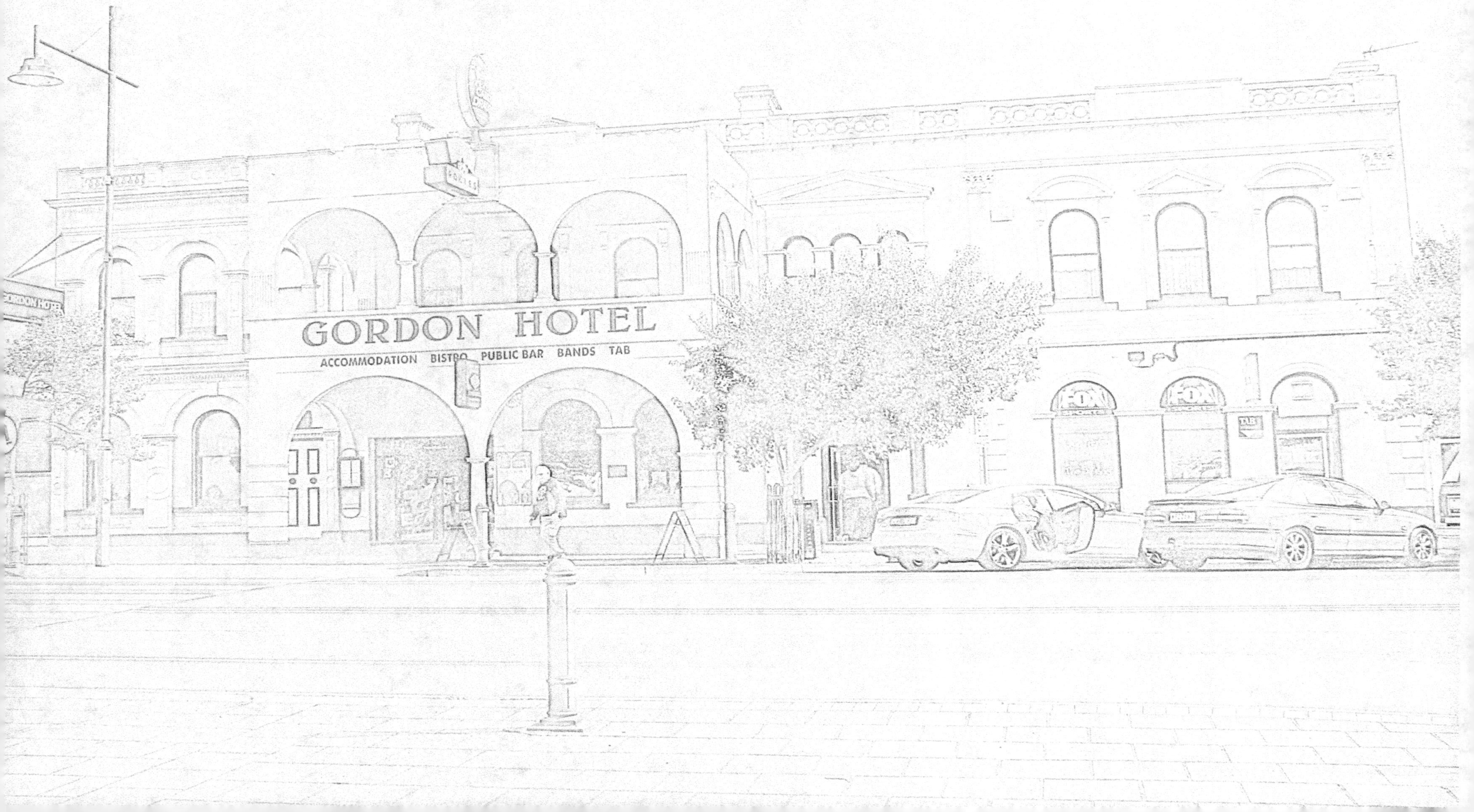
GORDON HOTEL
ACCOMMODATION BISTRO PUBLIC BAR BANDS TAB
GORDON HOTEL

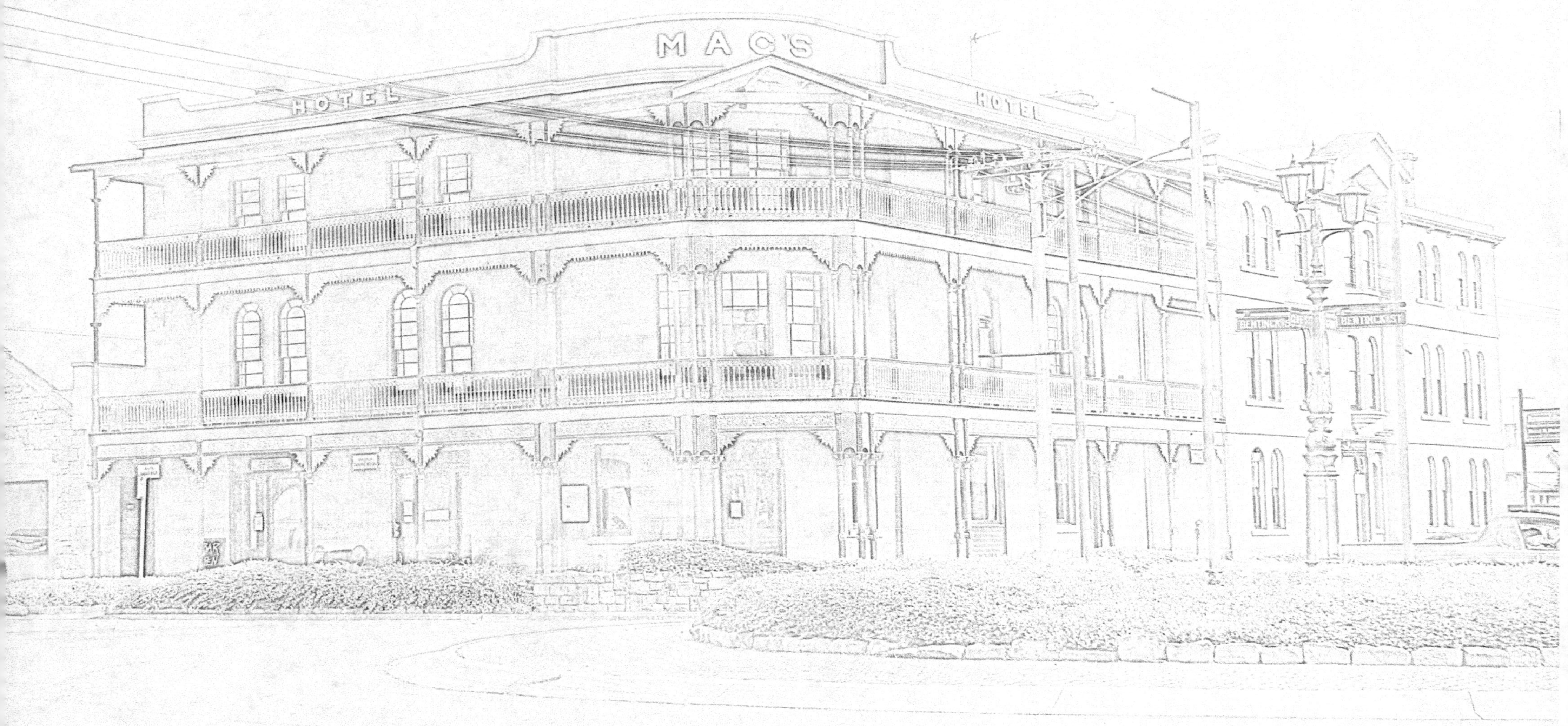
MAC'S
HOTEL
HOTEL
BENTINCK ST
BENTINCK ST

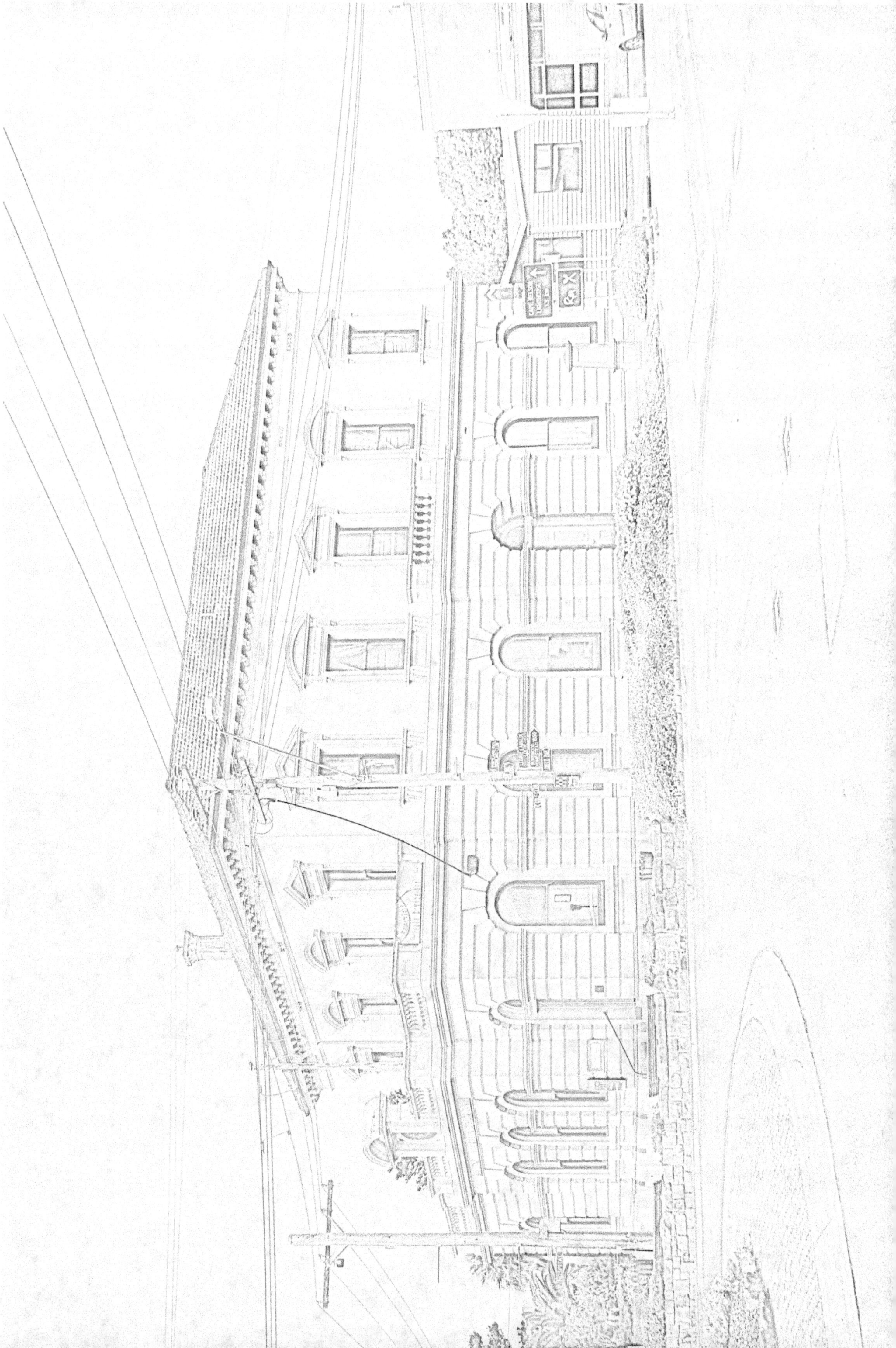

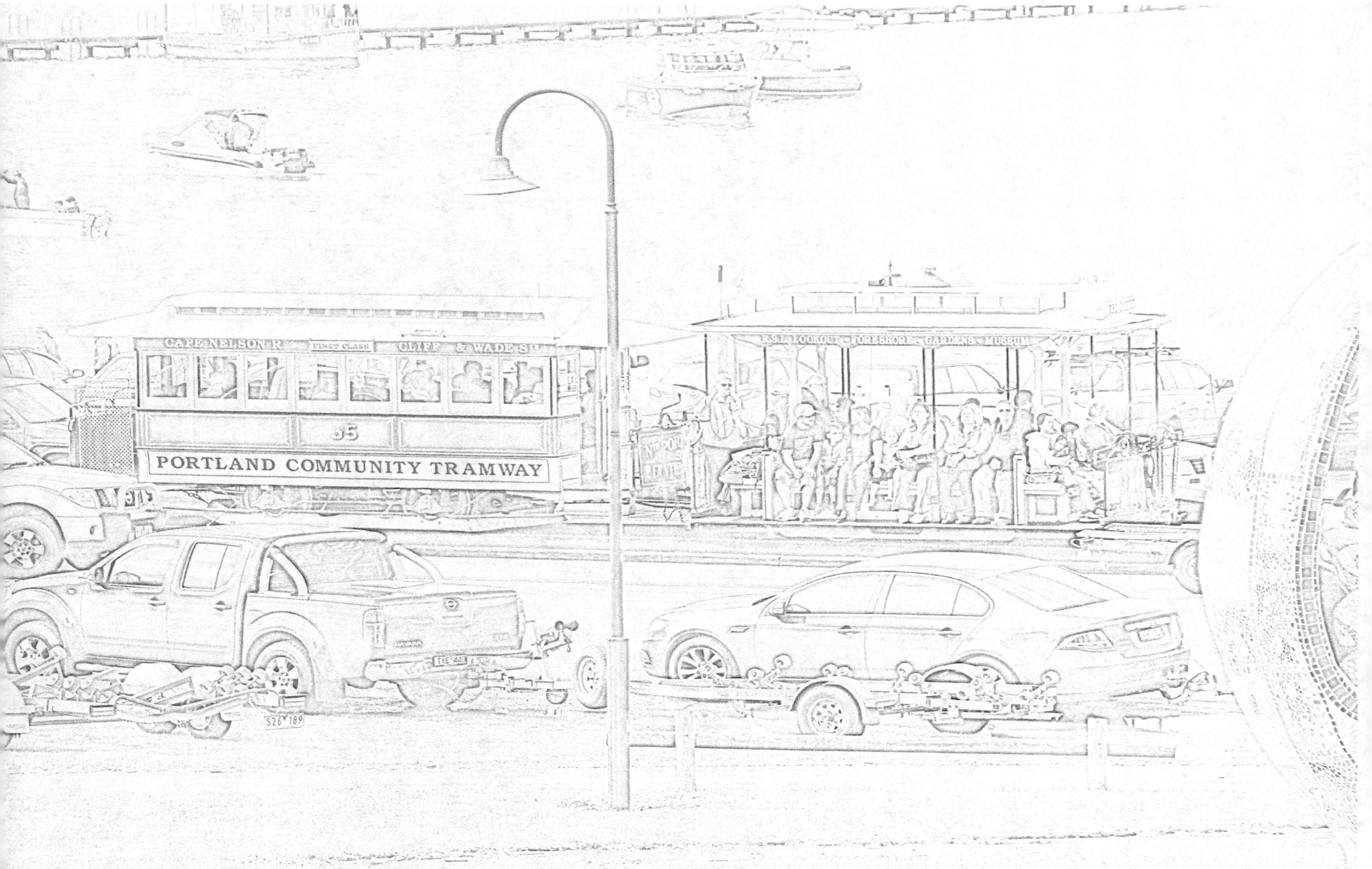
CAPE NELSON RD
FIRST CLASS
CLIFF & WADE STS
35
PORTLAND COMMUNITY TRAMWAY
R.S.L. LOOKOUT - FORESHORE - GARDENS - MUSEUM
S26 189

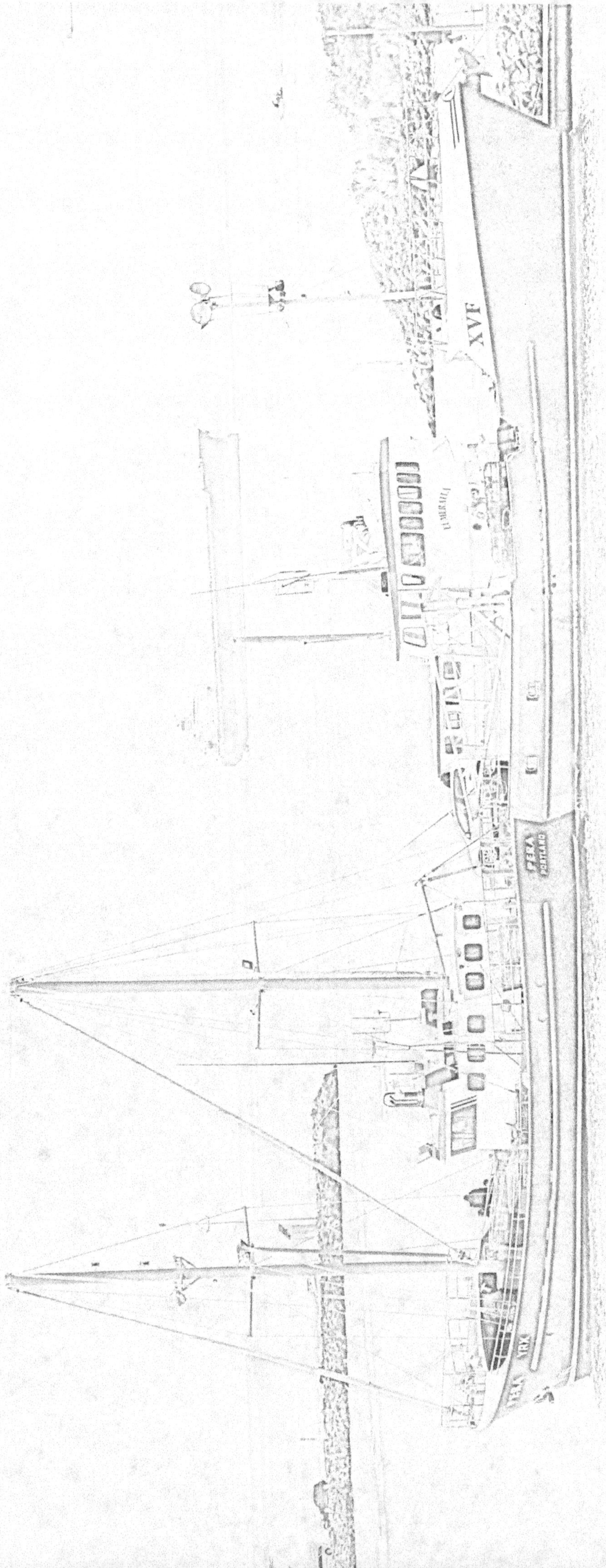
XVF

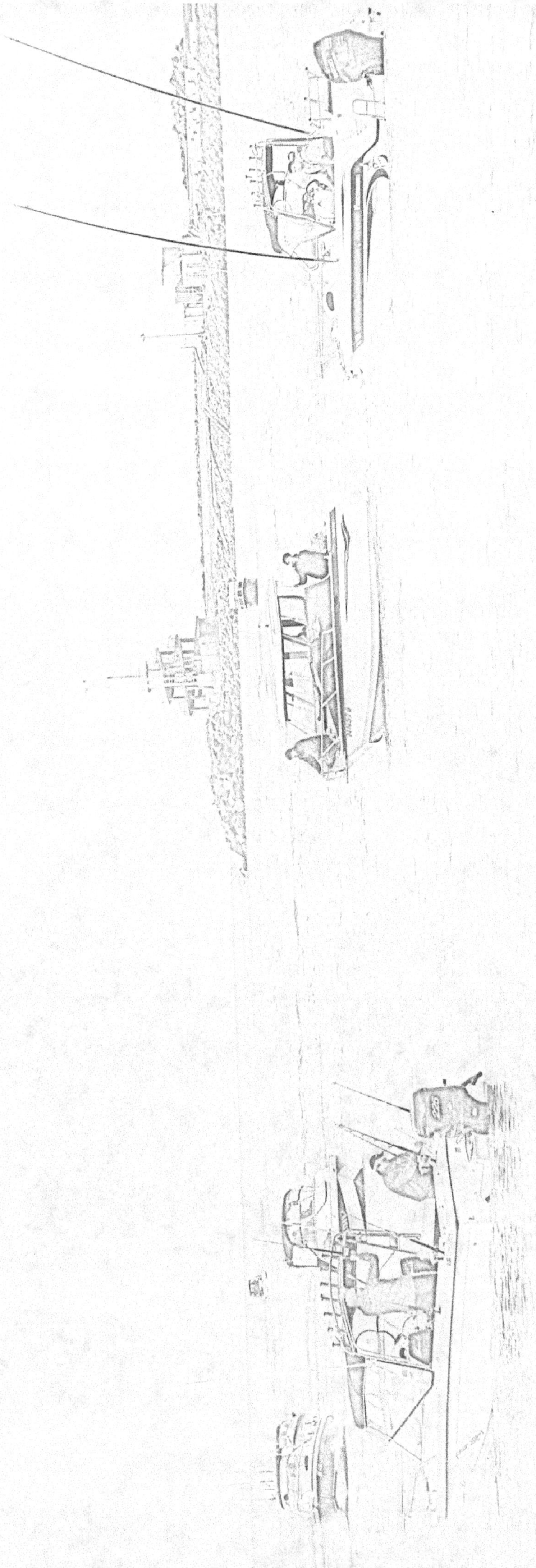

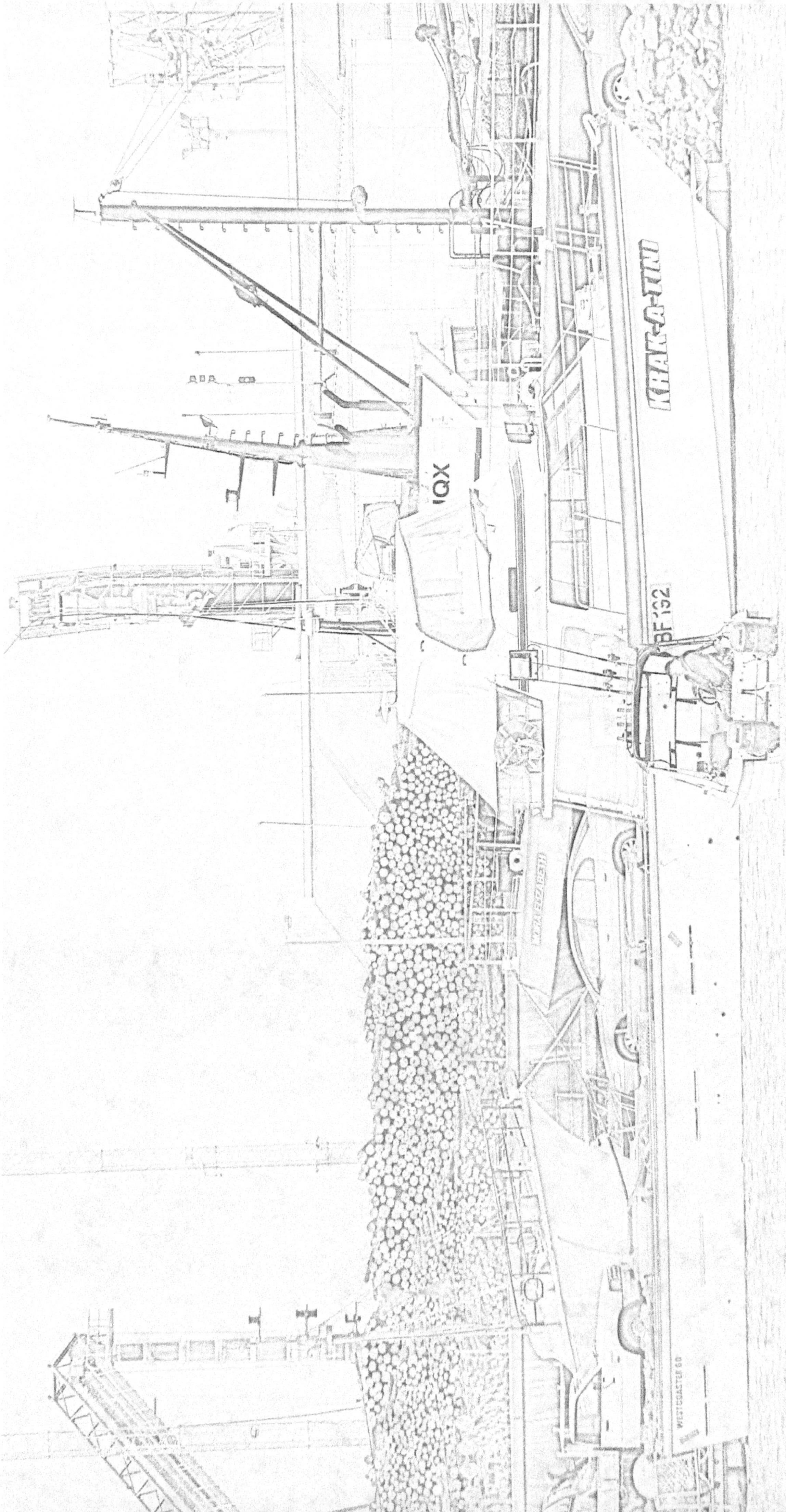
KRAK-A-TINI
BF 132
IQX

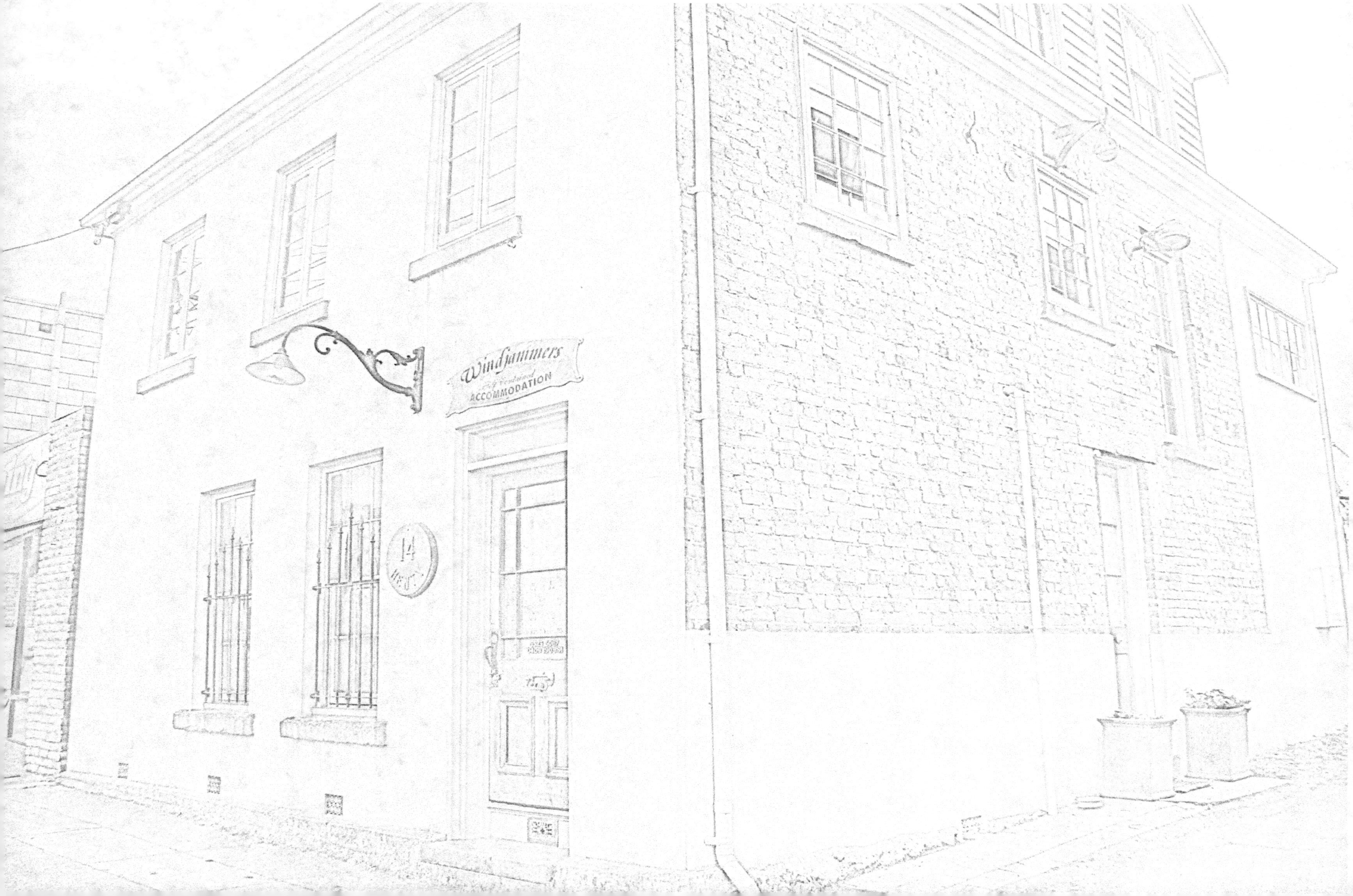
Windjammers
ACCOMMODATION
14

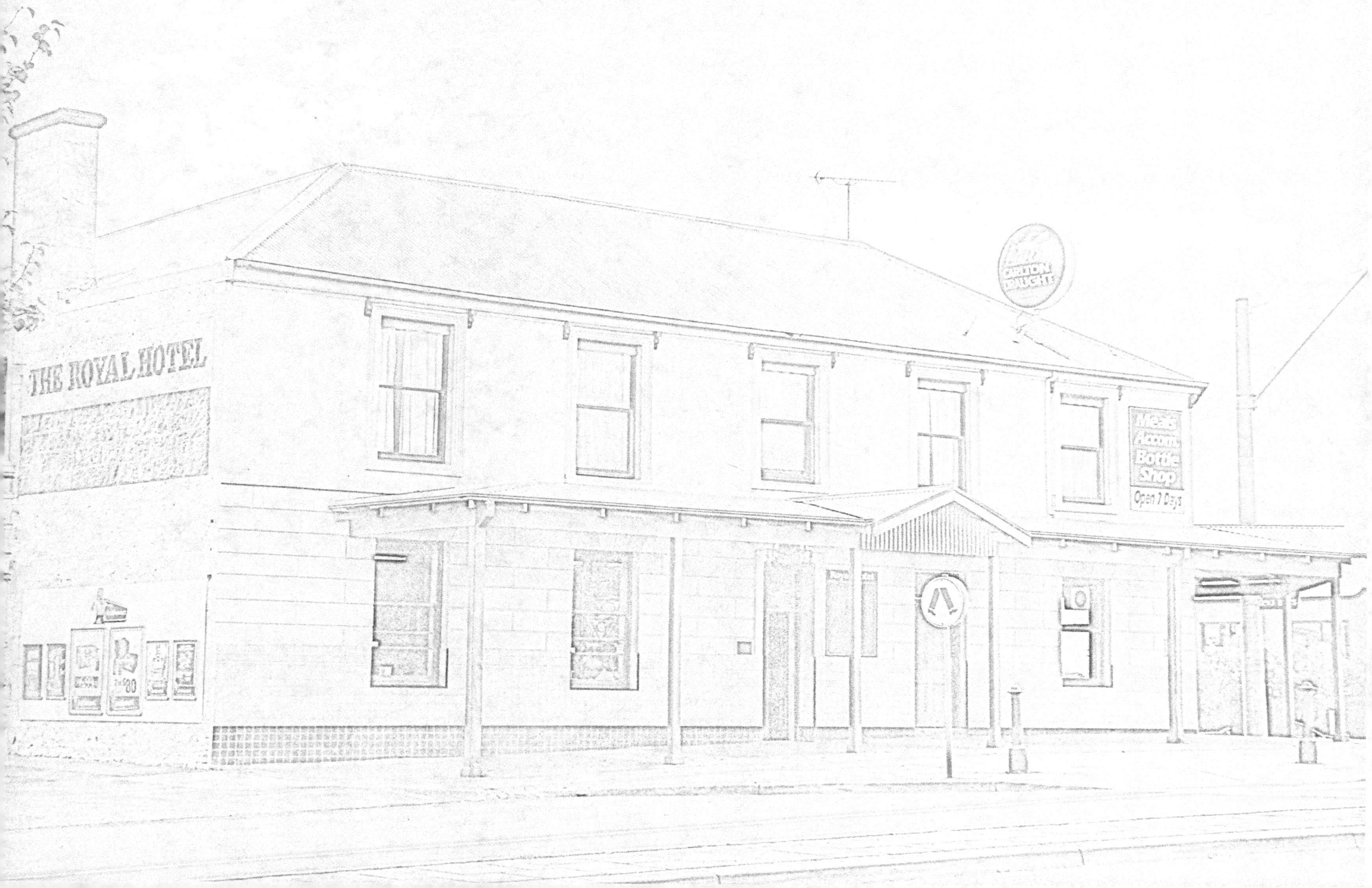
THE ROYAL HOTEL
Carlton Draught
Meals
Accom.
Bottle Shop
Open 7 Days

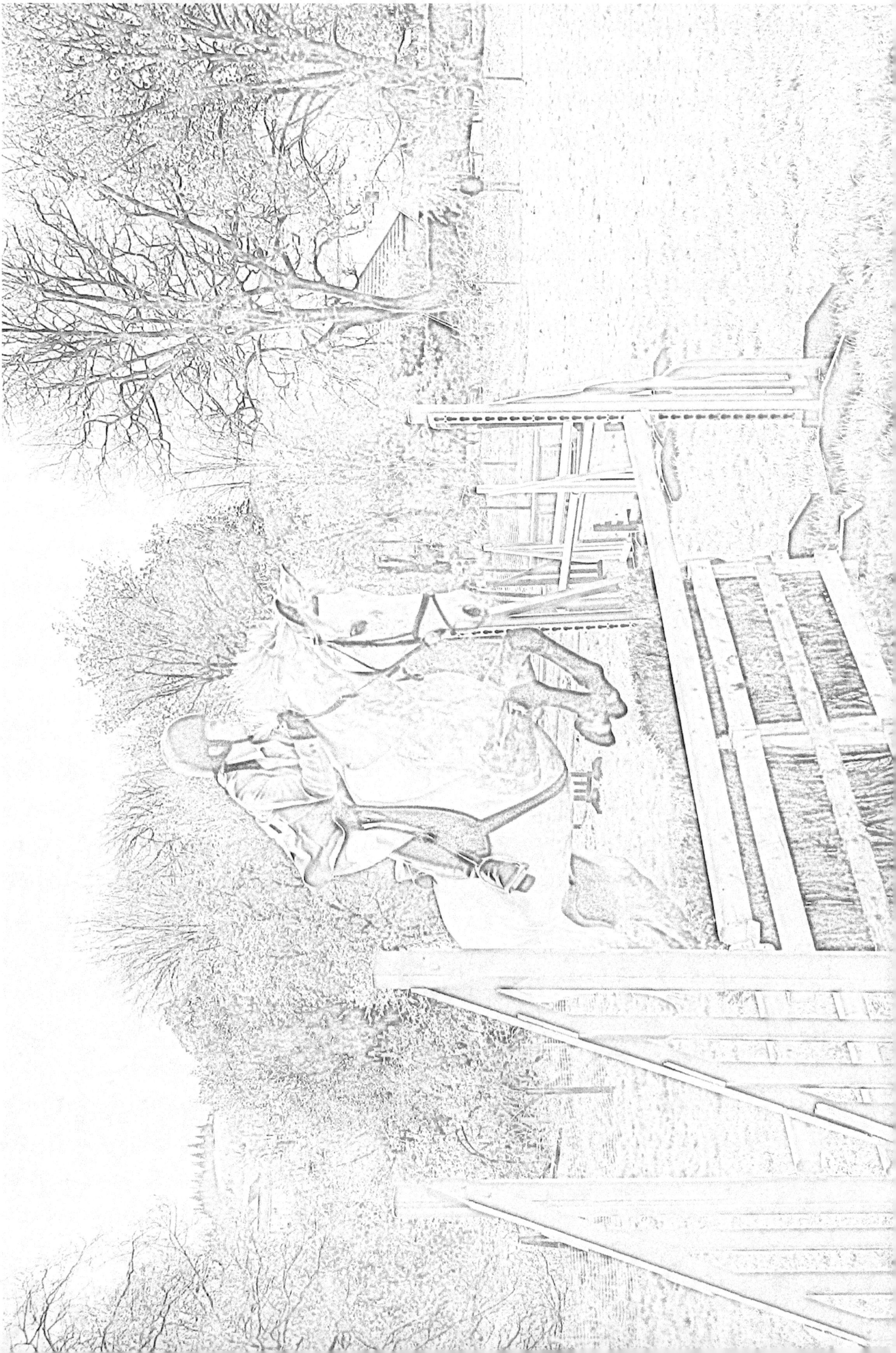

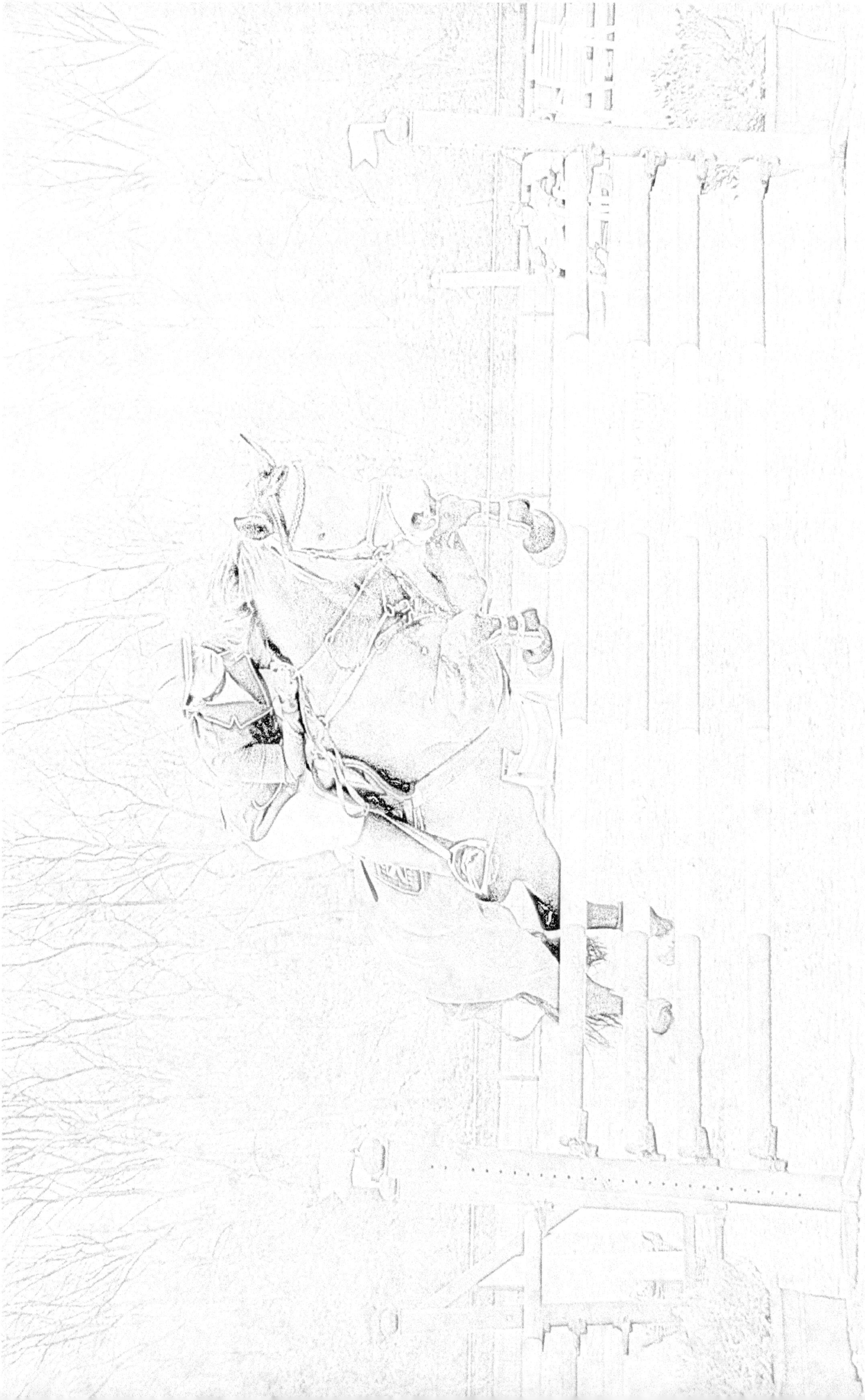

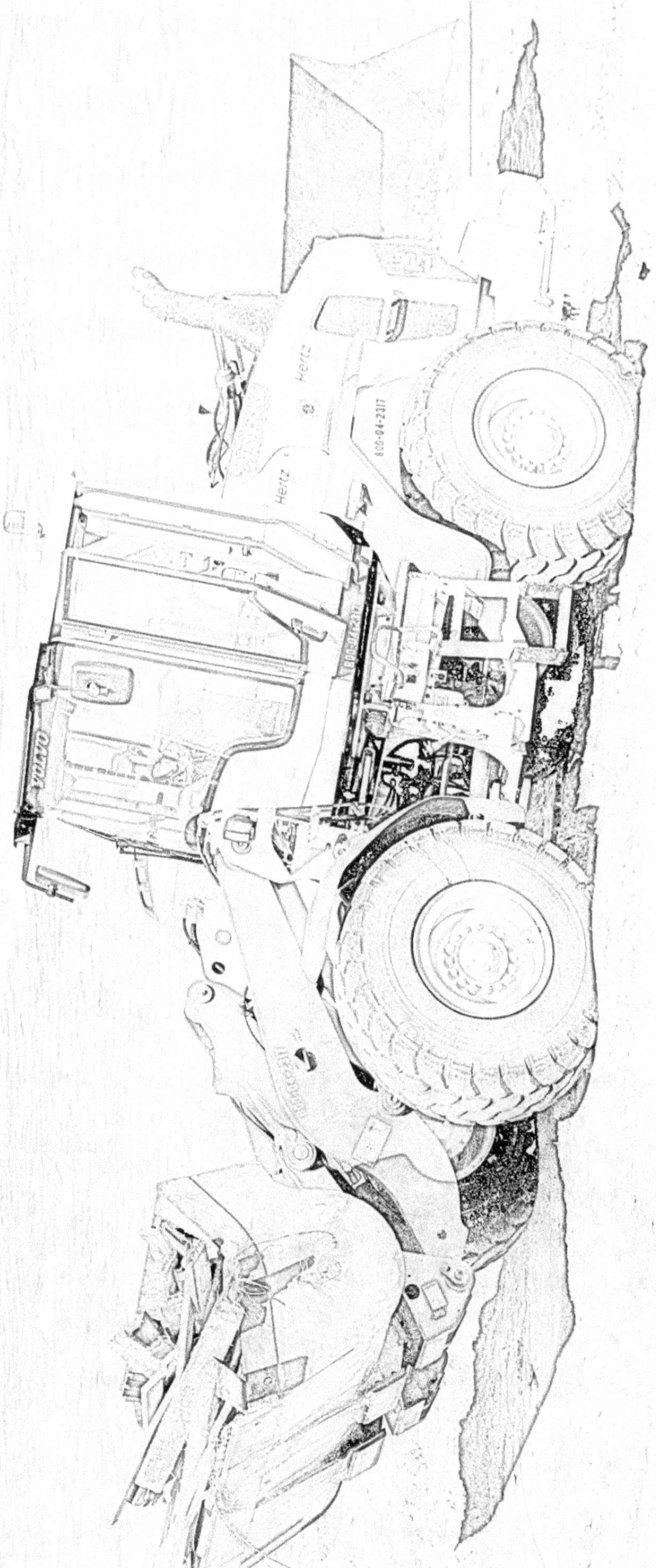
Hertz
800-04-2317
Hertz

Big Mallee Bird

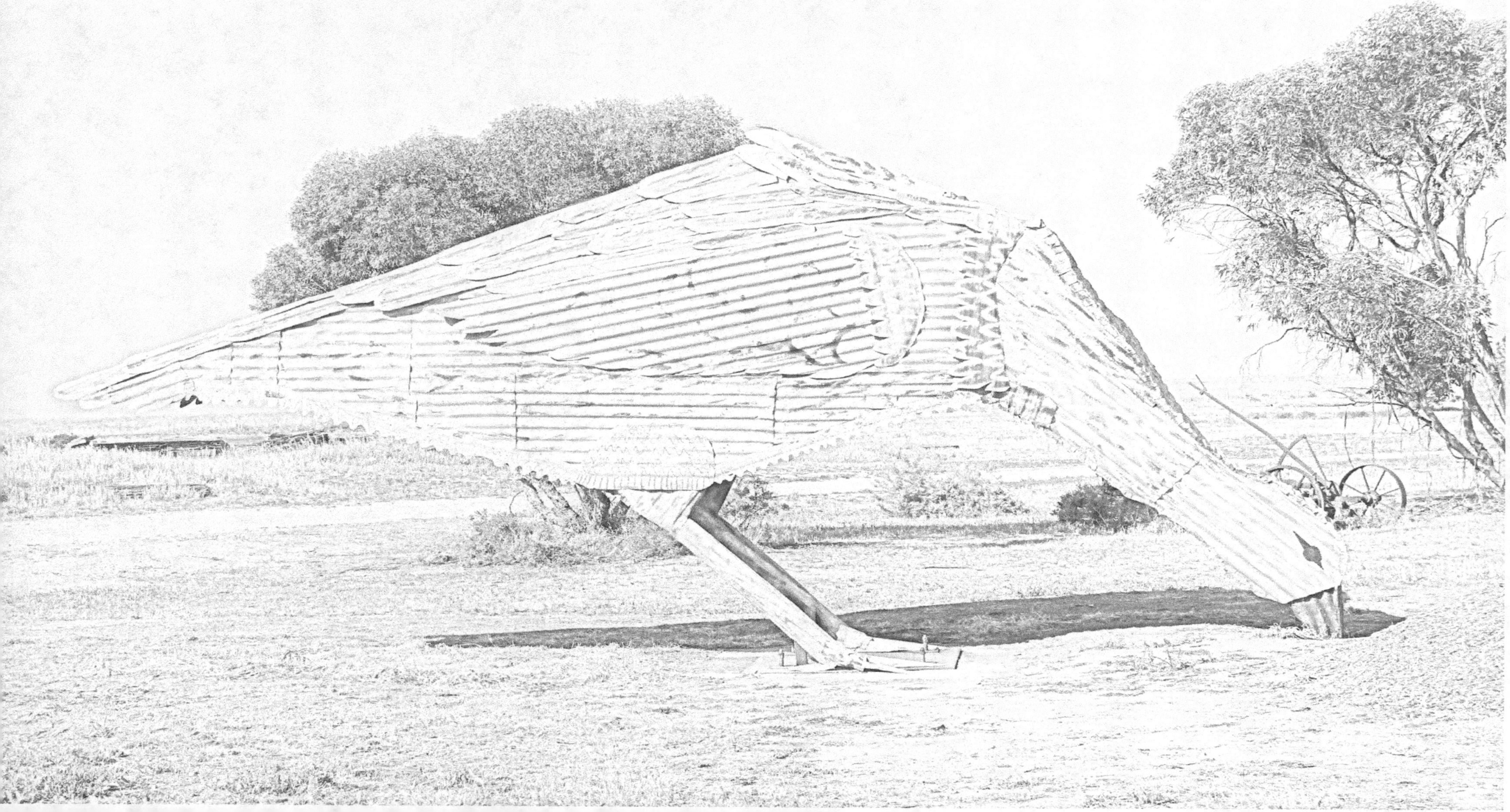

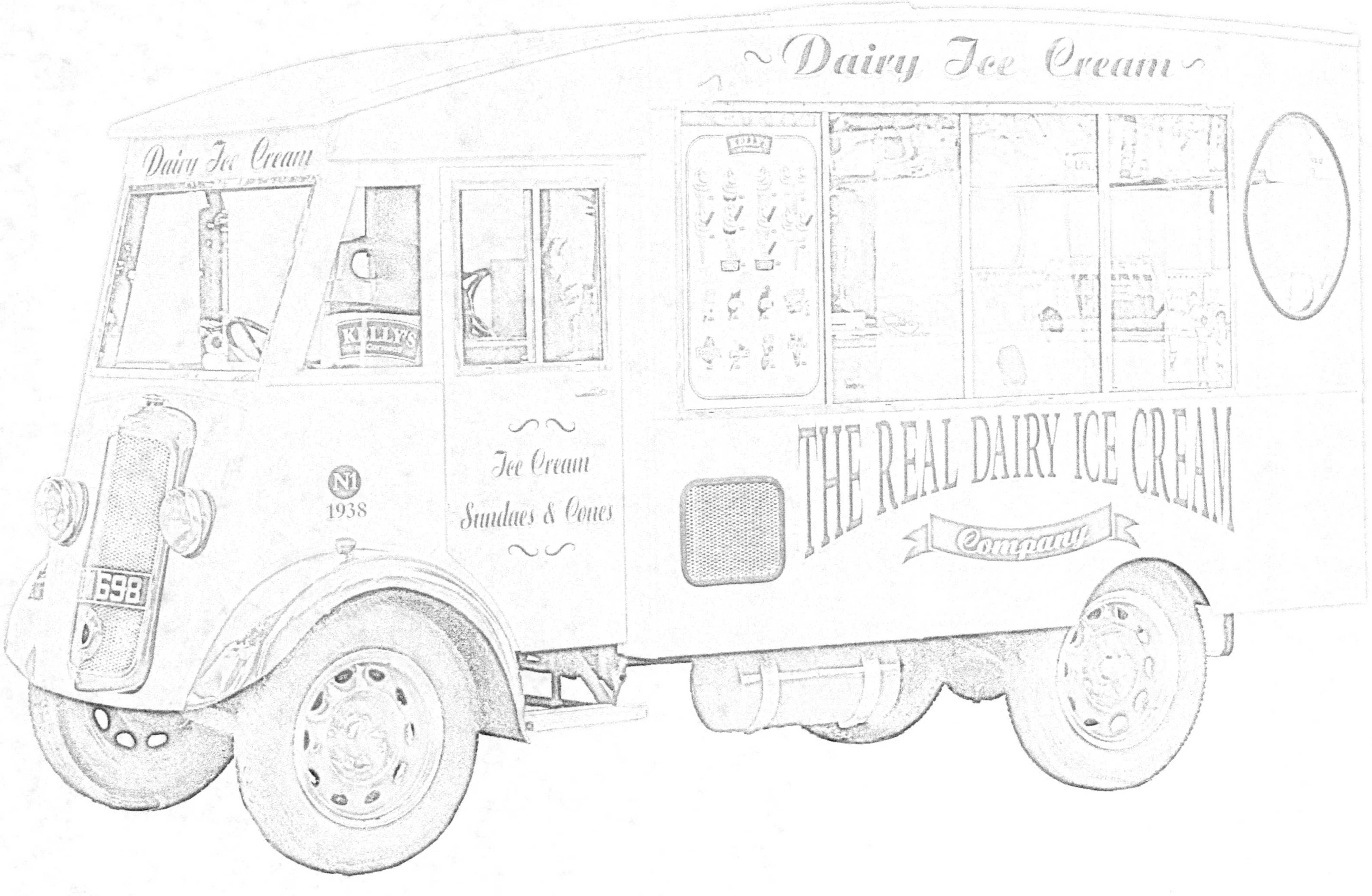
Dairy Ice Cream
Dairy Ice Cream
KELLY'S
N1
1938
Ice Cream
Sundaes & Cones
THE REAL DAIRY ICE CREAM
Company
1698

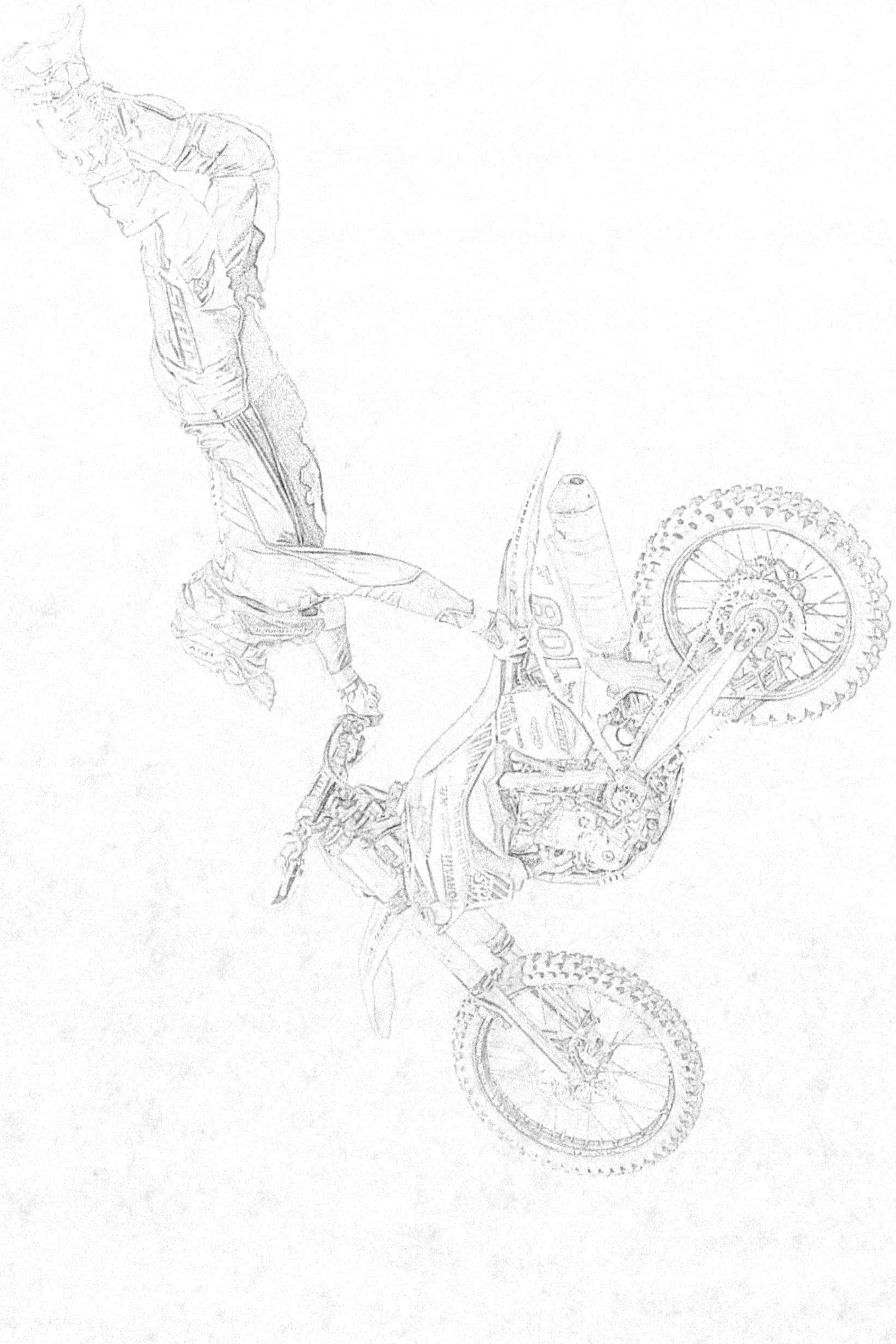

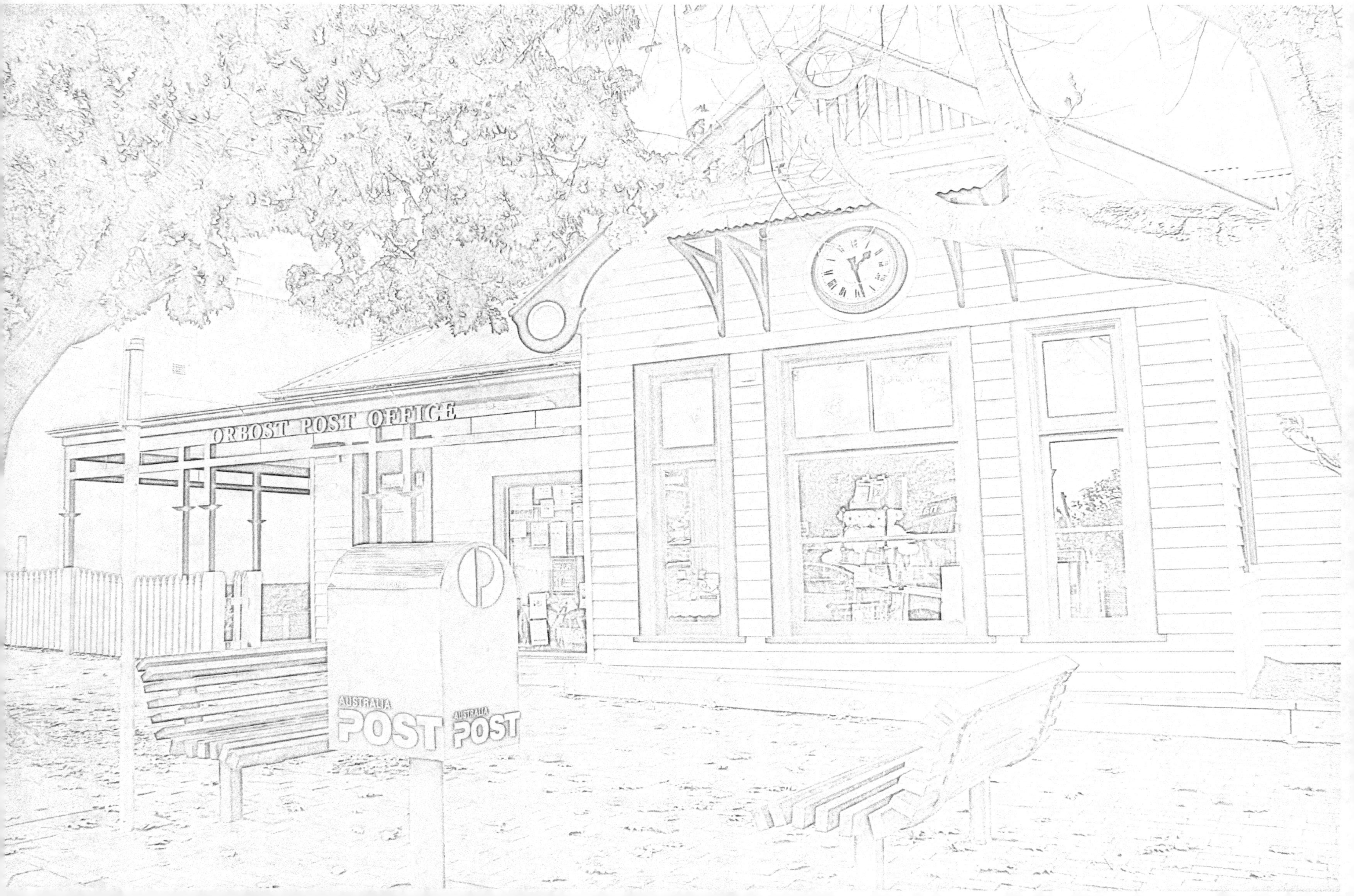
ORBOST POST OFFICE
AUSTRALIA POST
AUSTRALIA POST

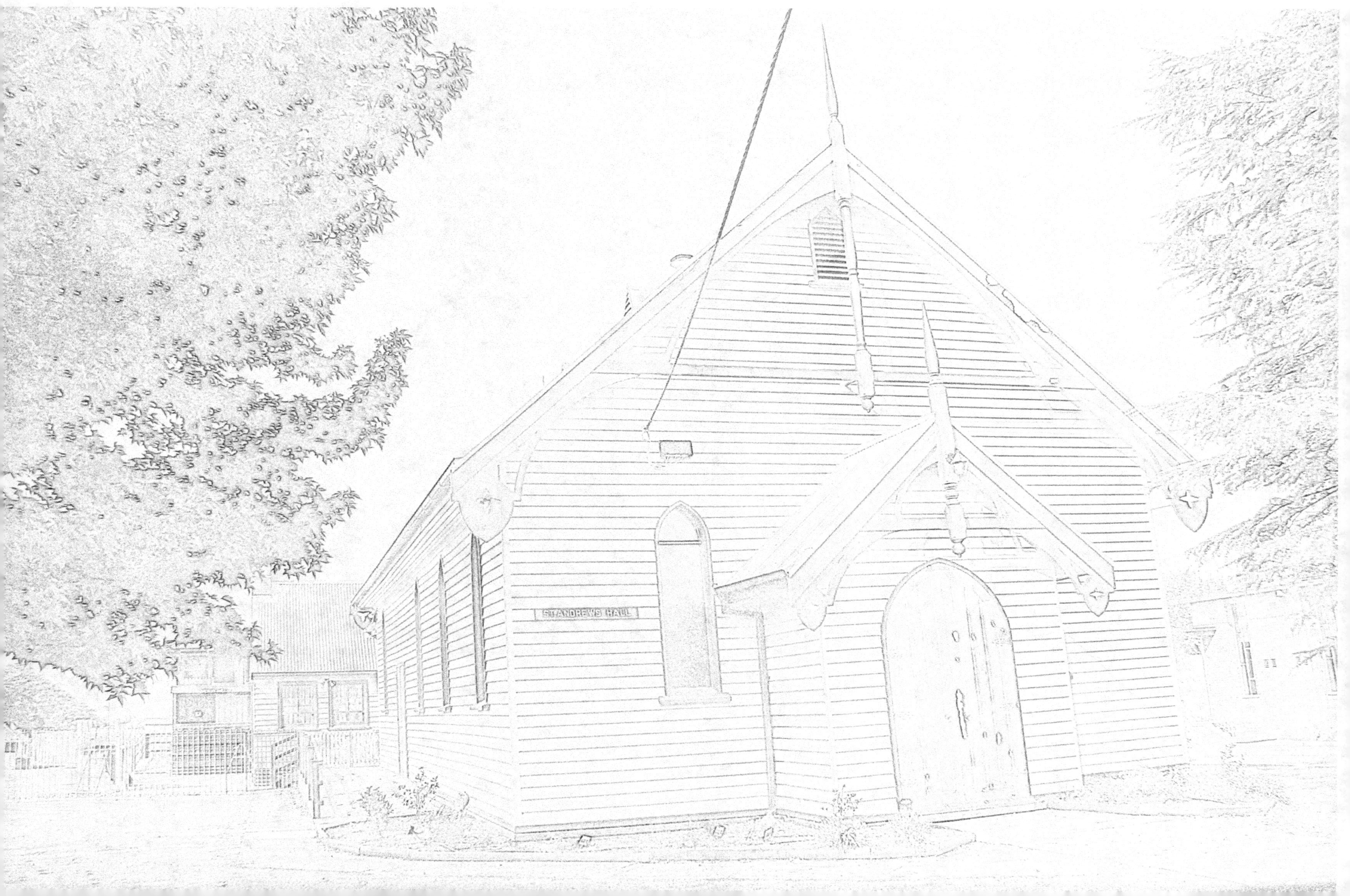
ST ANDREWS HALL

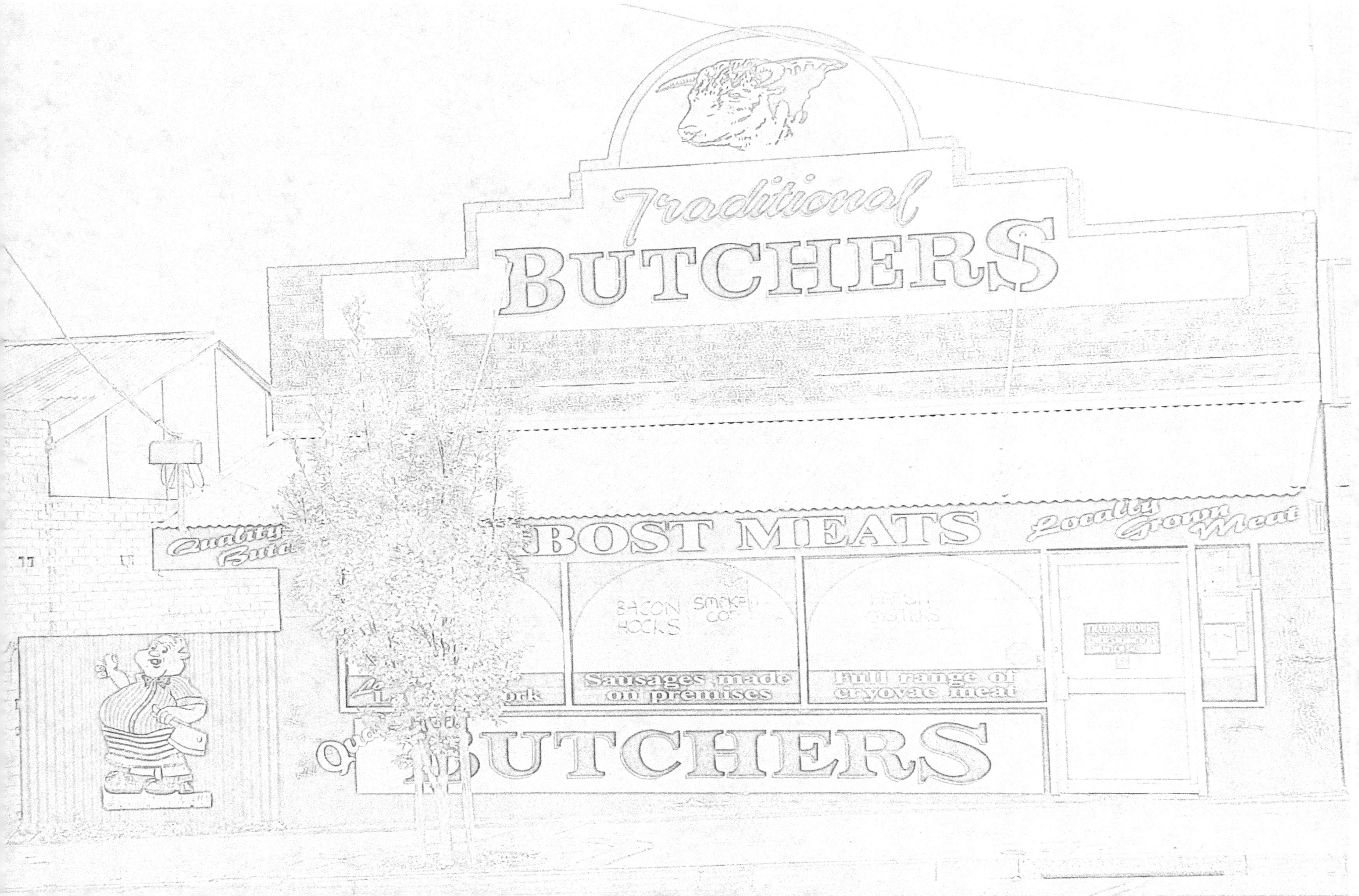
Traditional
BUTCHERS
BOST MEATS
Locally Grown Meat
BACON HOCKS
Sausages made on premises
Full range of cryovac meat
BUTCHERS

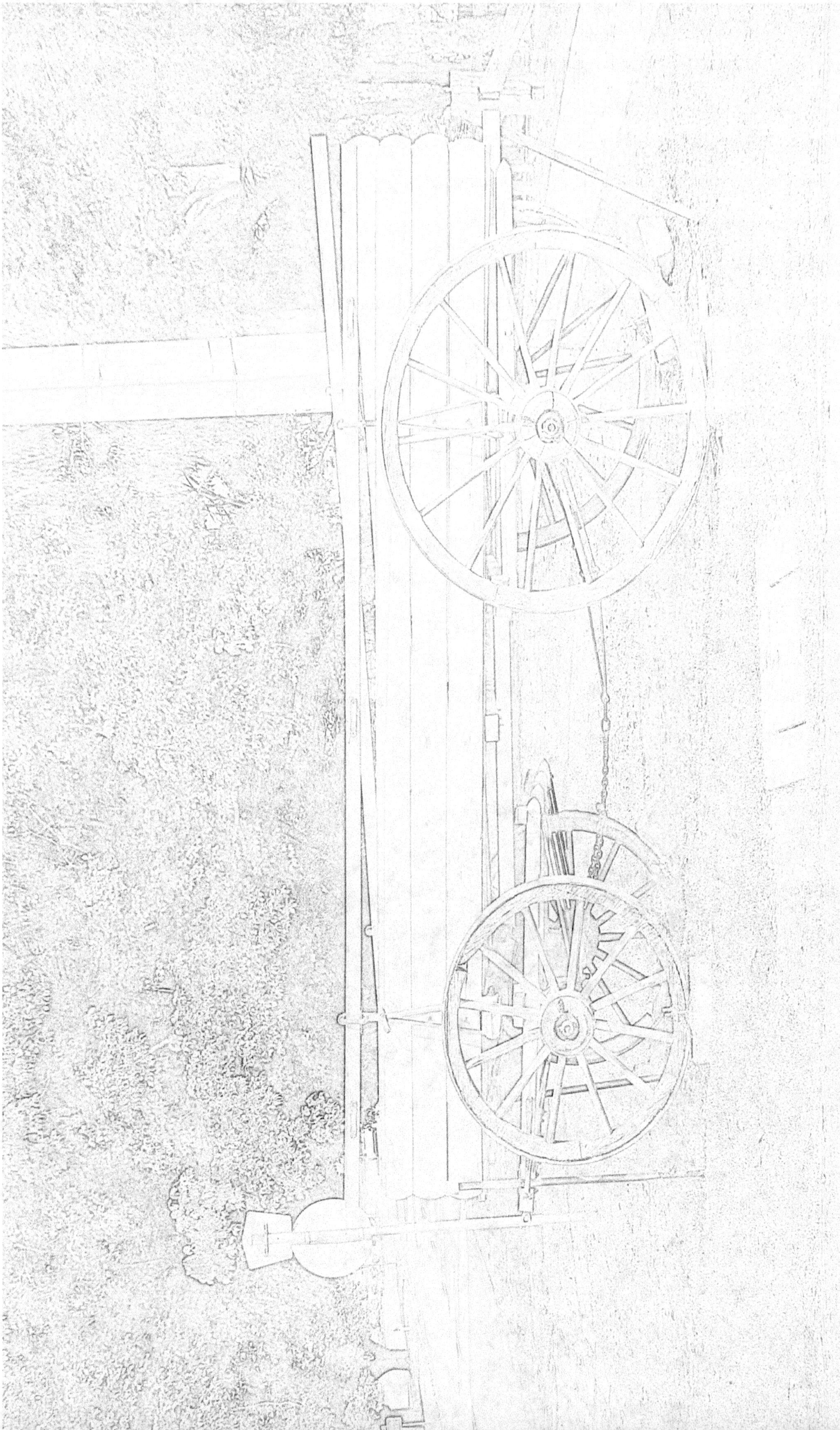

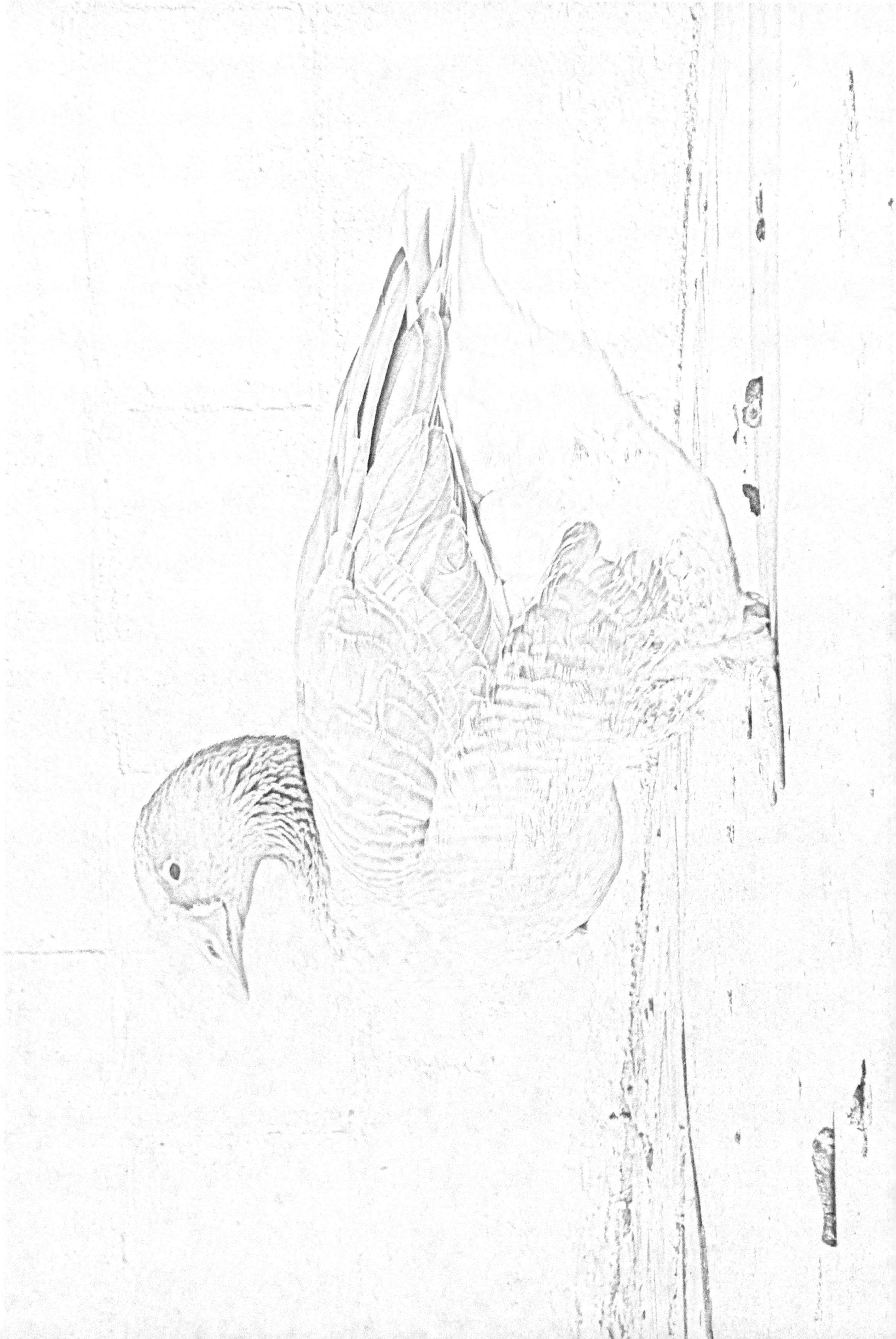

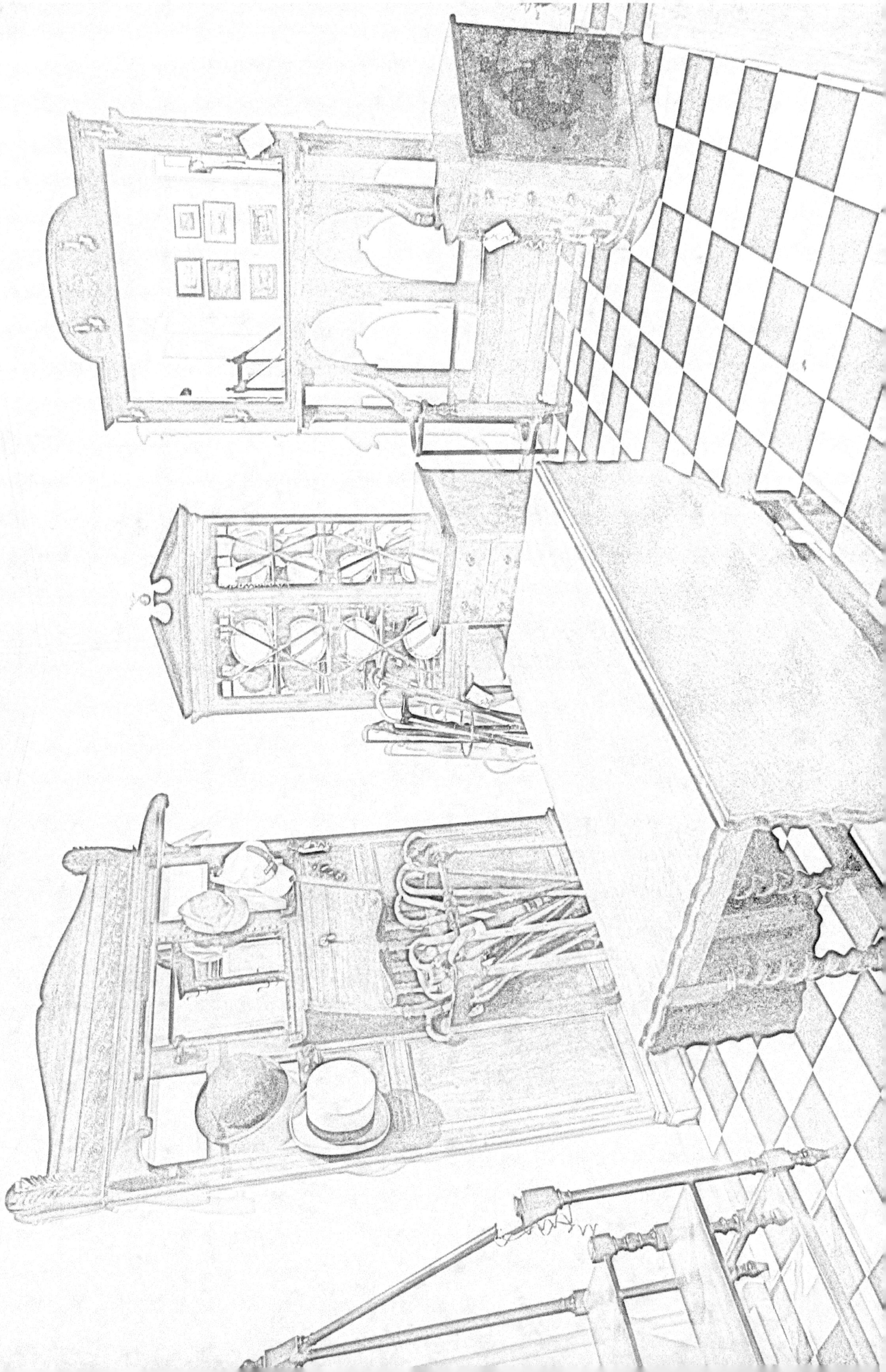

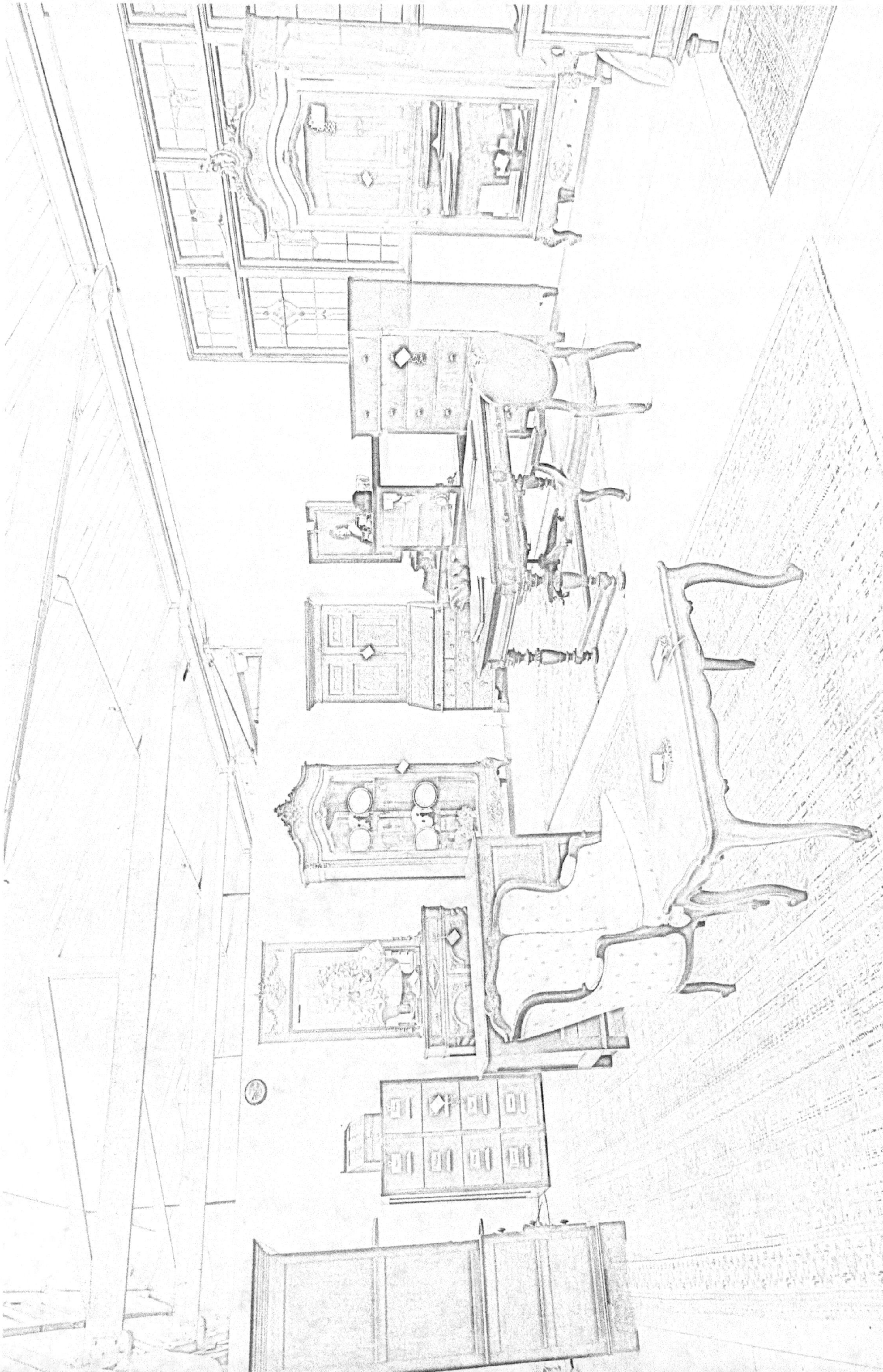

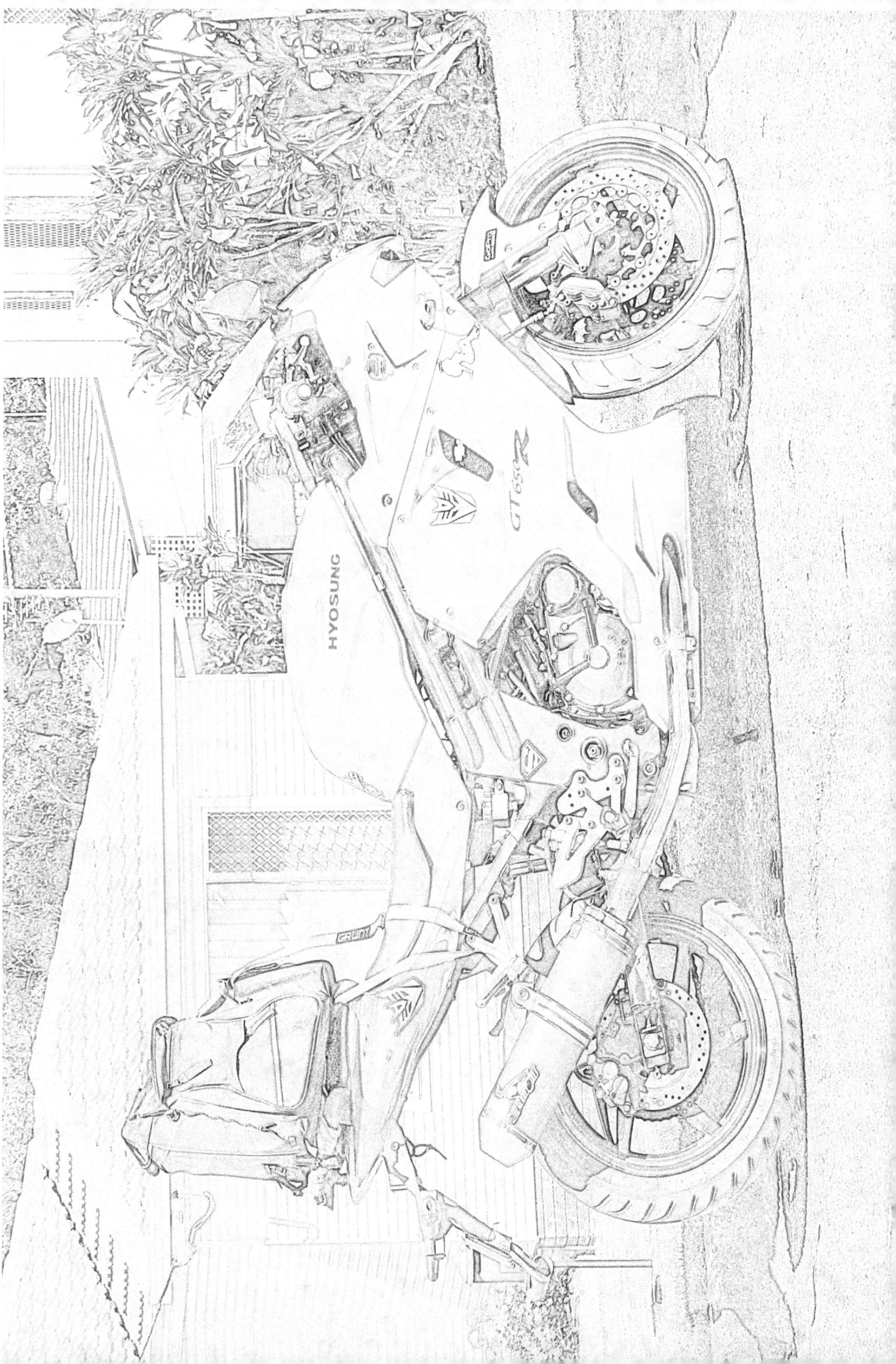
HYOSUNG
GT650R

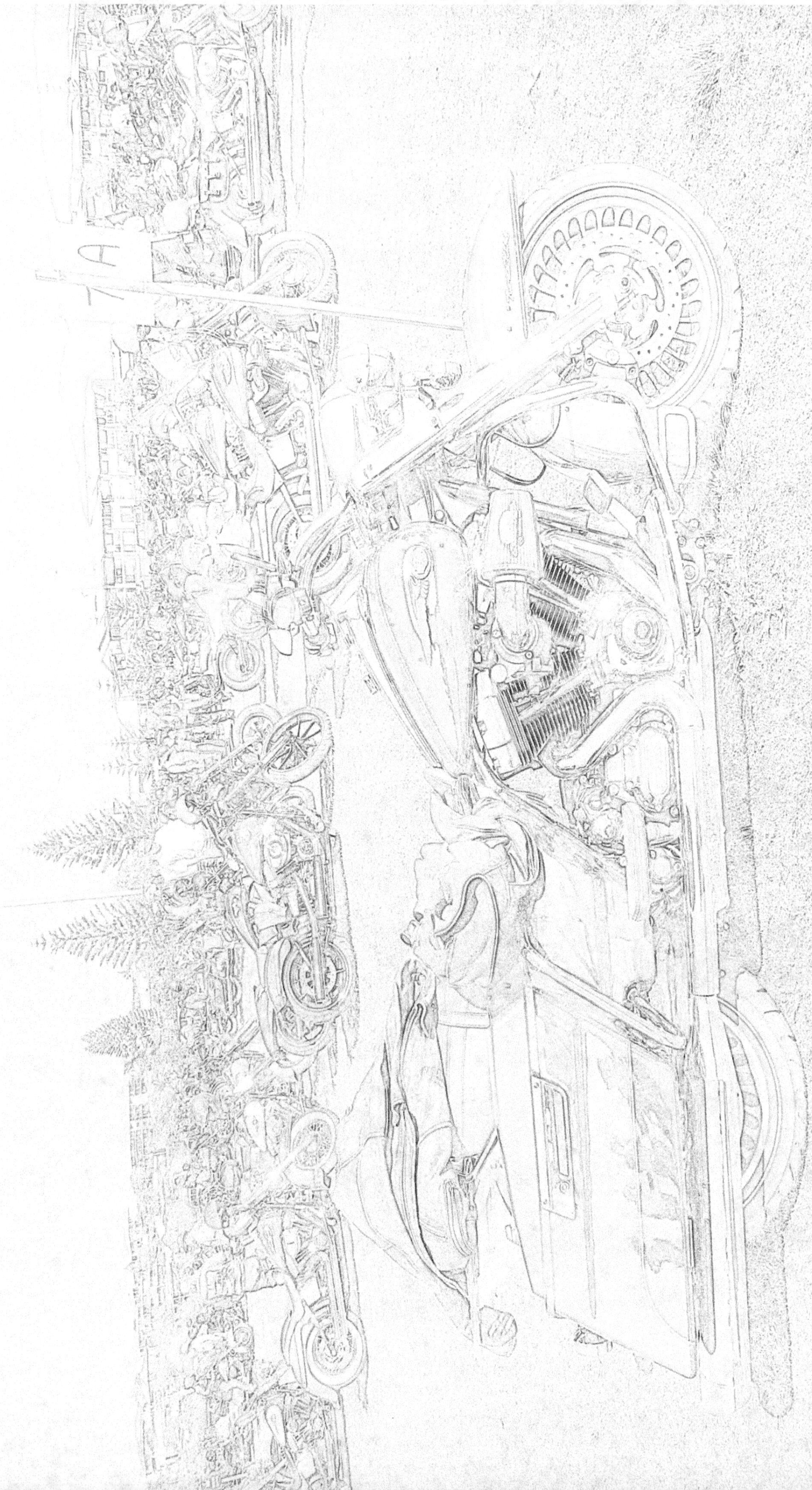

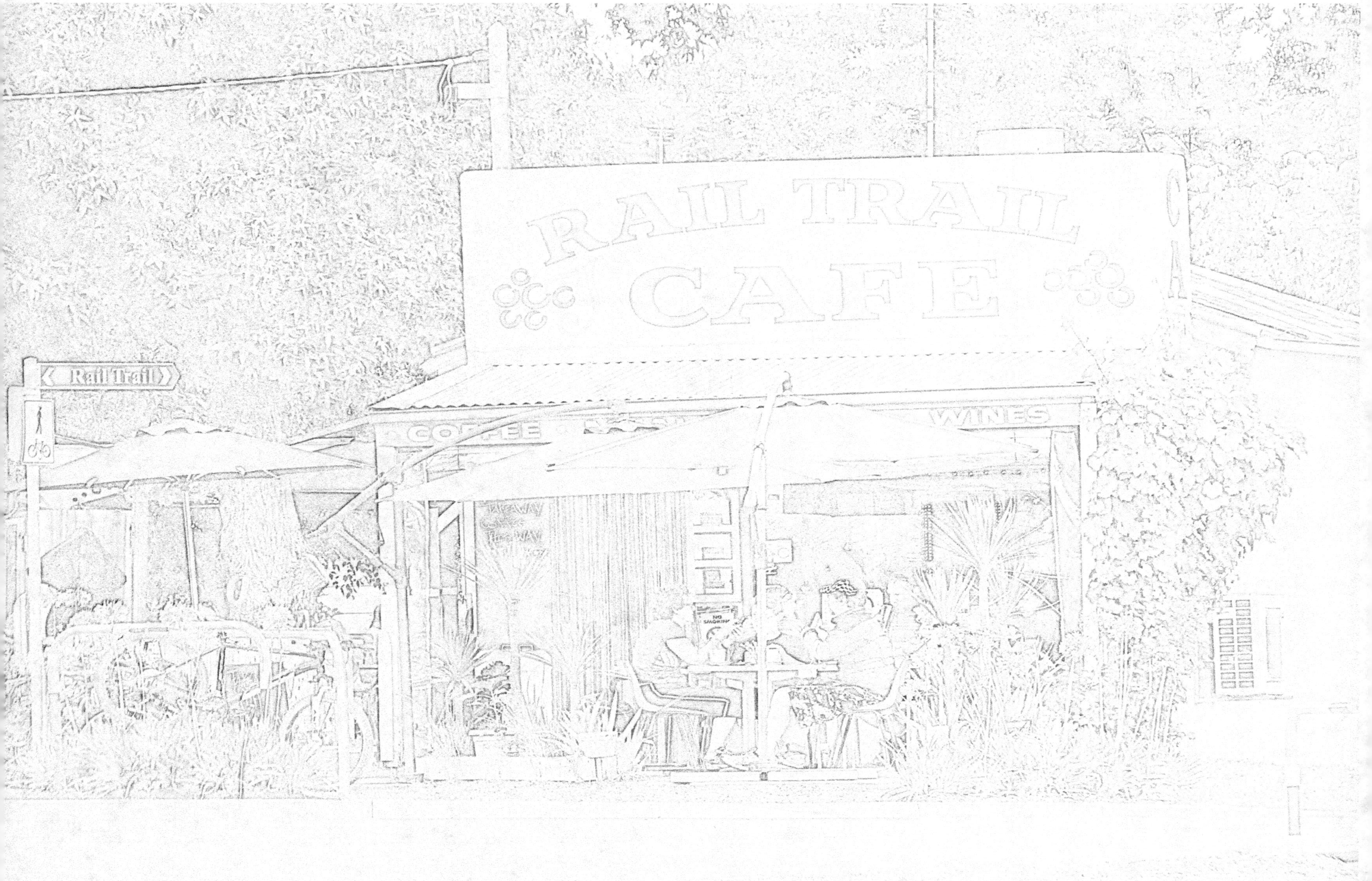
RAIL TRAIL
CAFE
Rail Trail
COFFEE
WINES
NO SMOKING

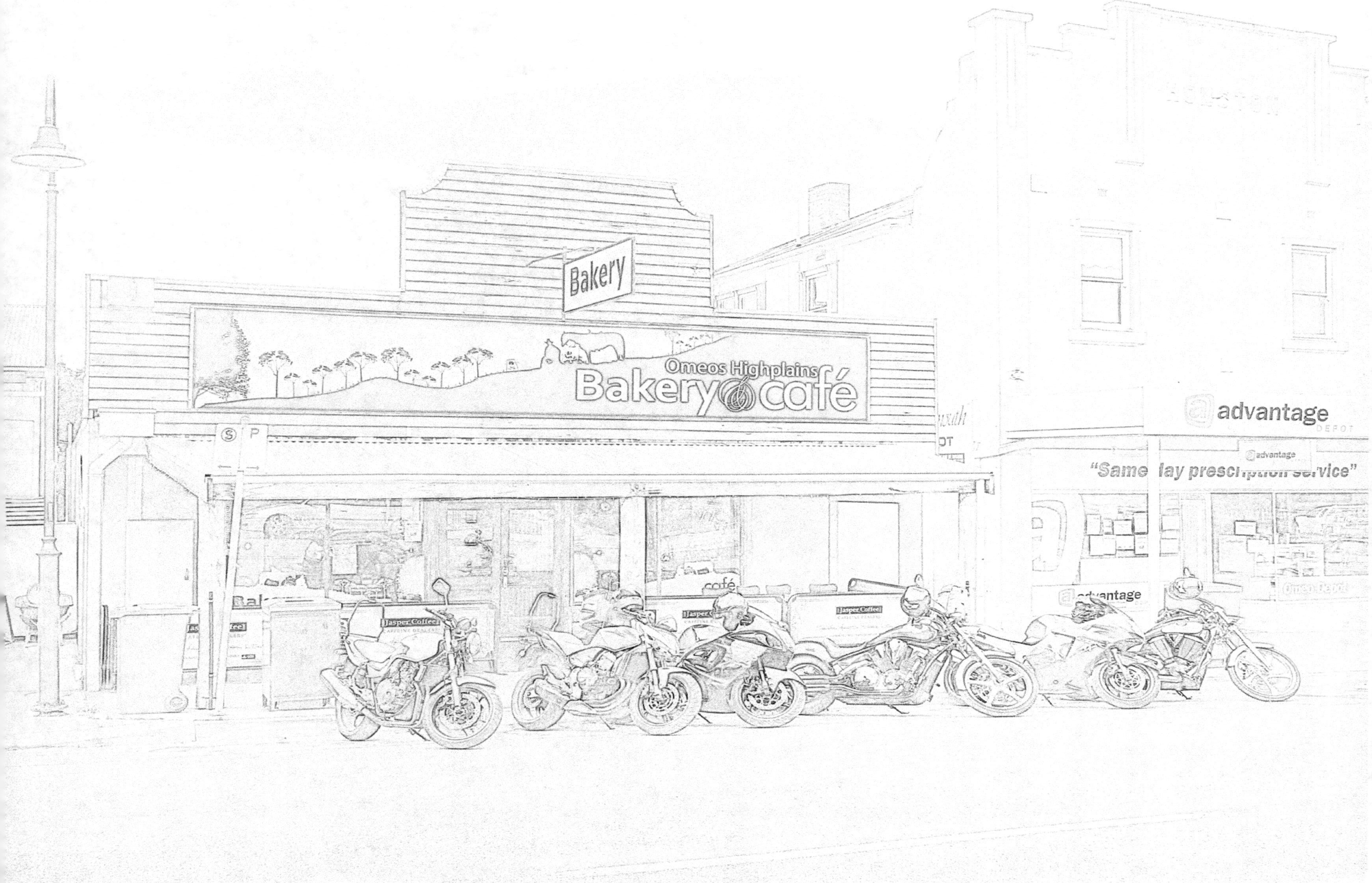
Bakery
Omeos Highplains
Bakery café
advantage
DEPOT
"Same day prescription service"
Jasper Coffee
café
advantage
Omeo Depot

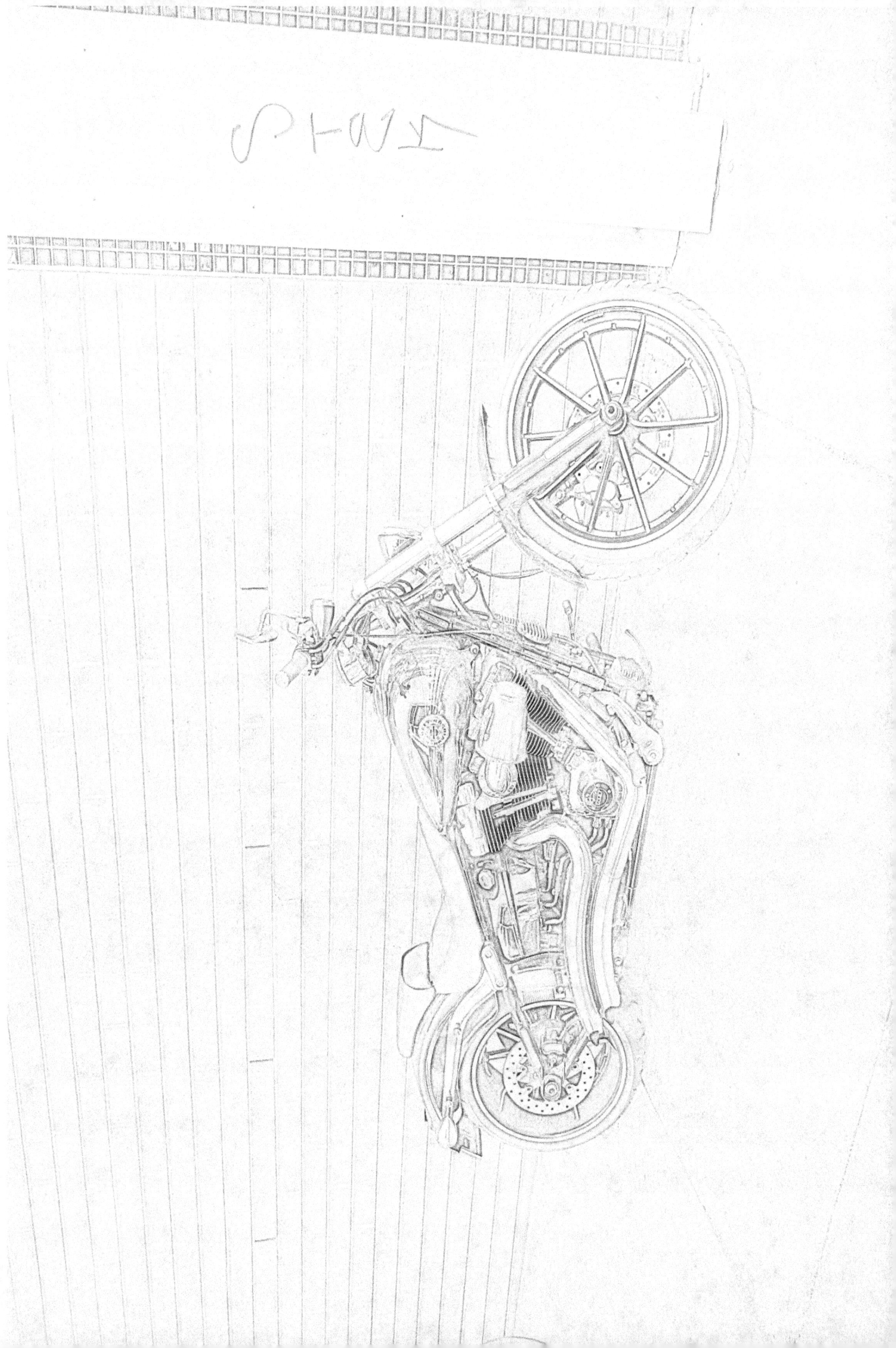

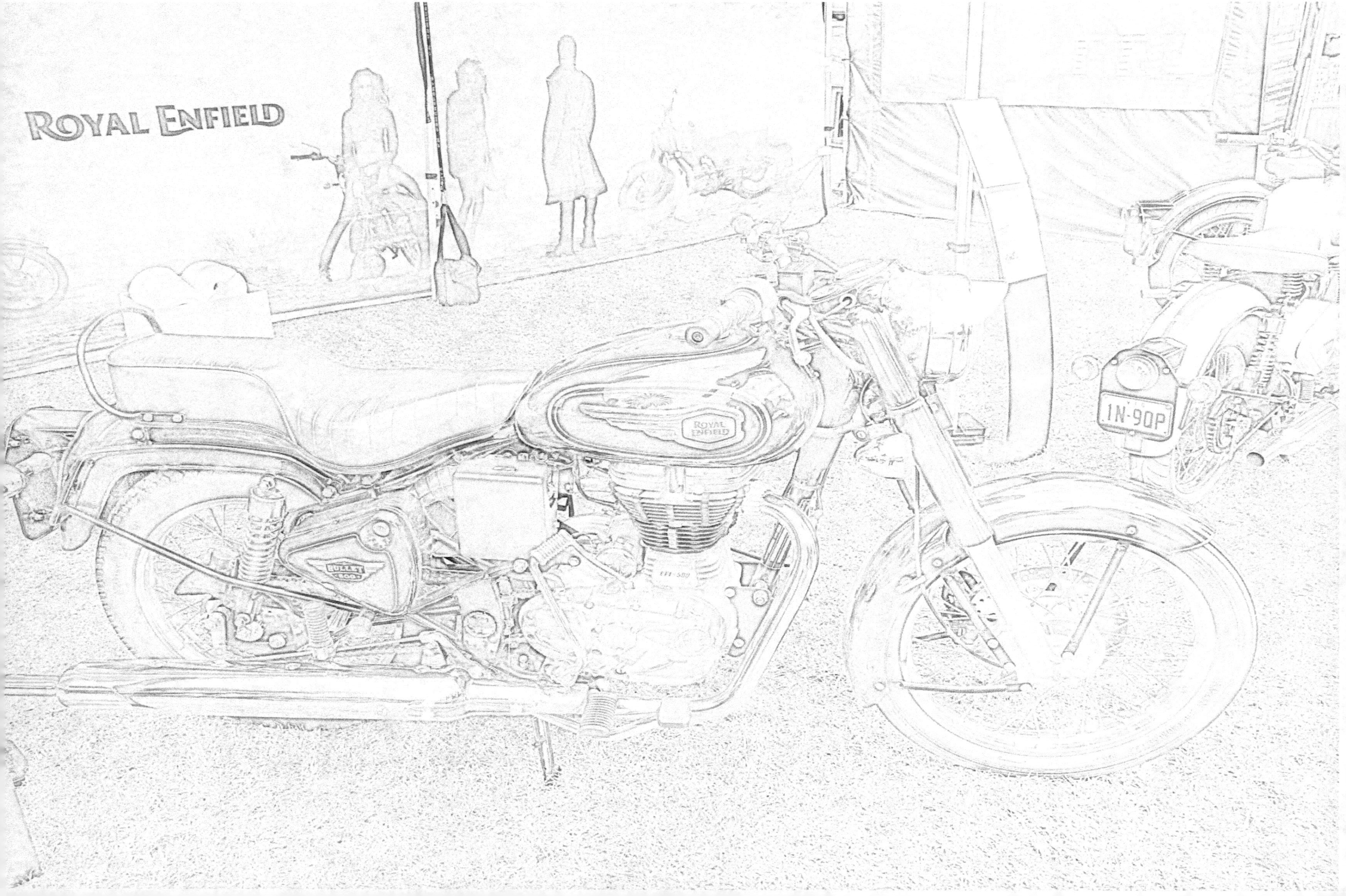
ROYAL ENFIELD
ROYAL ENFIELD
BULLET 500
1N-90P

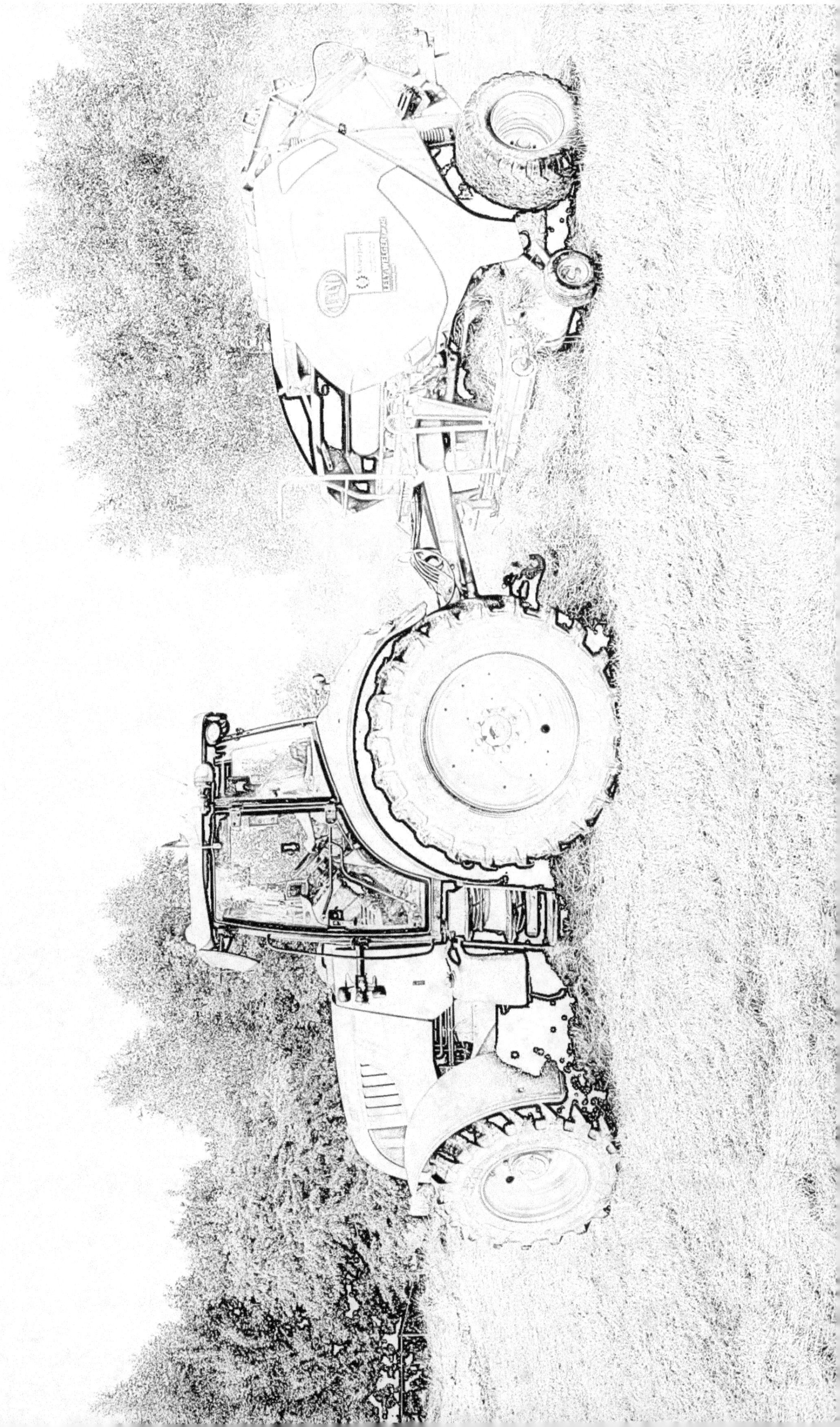

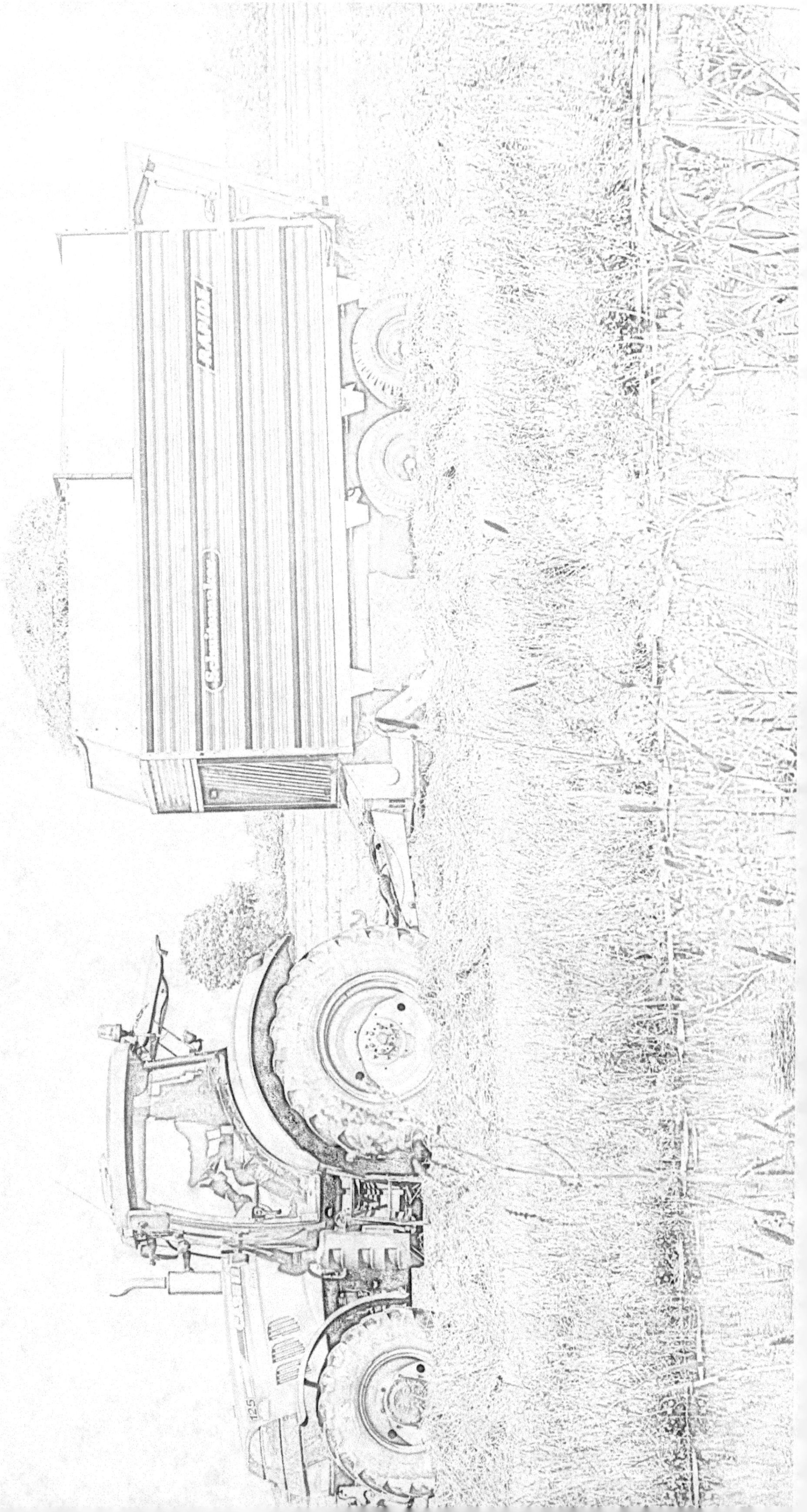

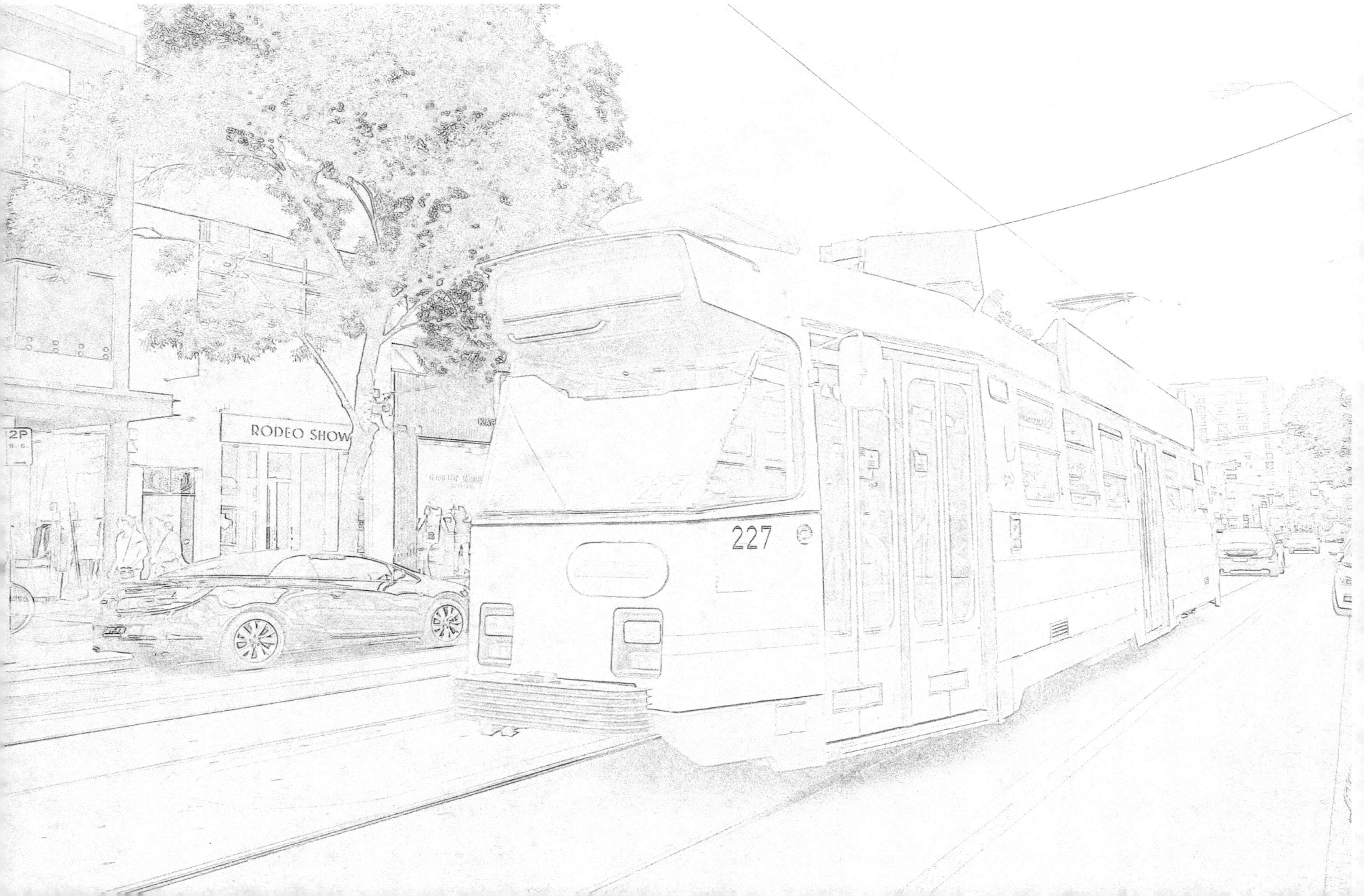
2P
RODEO SHOW
227

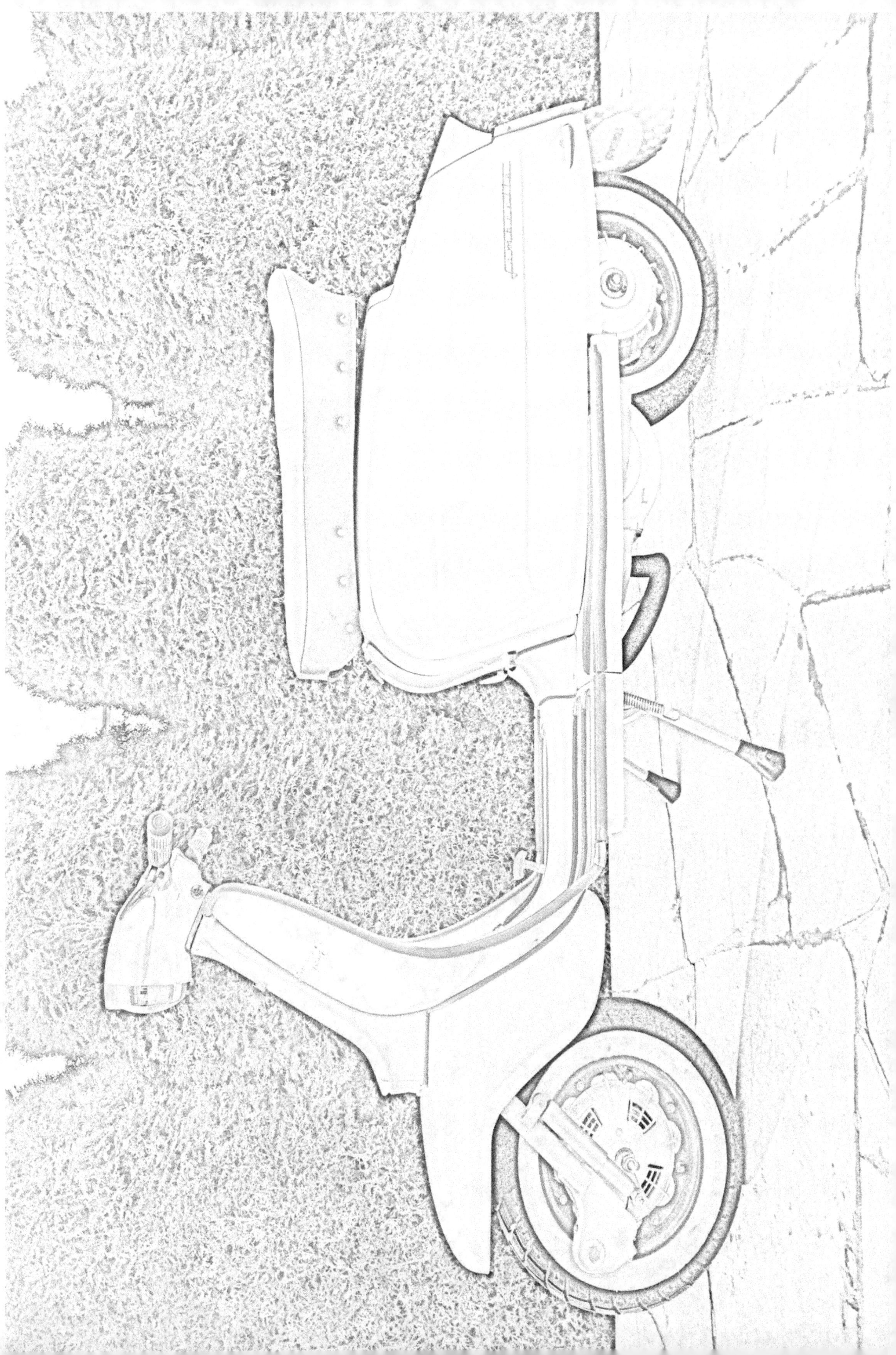

www.ingramcontent.com/pod-product-compliance
Lightning Source LLC
Chambersburg PA
CBHW081052180526
45170CB00005B/1767